U0627072

Reading for the Citizen of the World
世界公民读本（文库）

FOUNDATIONS of DEMOCRACY

R G Reading for the Citizen of the World
世界公民读本（文库）

Foundations of Democracy

民主的基础丛书

主编 赵文彤

Authority

权威

〔美〕Center for Civic Education (公民教育中心) 著

刘小小 译

隐私
PRIVACY

正义
JUSTICE

权威
AUTHORITY

责任
RESPONSIBILITY

金城出版社
GOLD WALL PRESS

FOUNDATIONS of DEMOCRACY

AUTHORITY PRIVACY RESPONSIBILITY JUSTICE

English Edition Copyright ©2009. Center for Civic Education. Calabasas, CA, USA.

著作权合同登记图字：B11002792-01-2011-3499

图书在版编目(CIP)数据

权威 /（美国）公民教育中心著；刘小小译. —北京
：金城出版社，2011.6
　　（世界公民读本文库/赵文彤主编）
　　书名原文：Authority
　　ISBN 978-7-80251-925-1

　　Ⅰ．①权… Ⅱ．①美… ②刘… Ⅲ．①权利-青年读
物②权利-少年读物 Ⅳ．①D911-49

　　中国版本图书馆CIP数据核字（2011）第075249号

权威

作　　者	CENTER FOR CIVIC EDUCATION（美国）公民教育中心
责任编辑	袁东旭
开　　本	710毫米×1000毫米 1/16
印　　张	18.5
字　　数	280千字
版　　次	2011年8月第1版 2011年8月第1次印刷
印　　刷	北京联兴华印刷厂
书　　号	ISBN 978-7-80251-925-1
定　　价	40.00元

出版发行	金城出版社 北京市朝阳区和平街11区37号楼 邮编：100013
发 行 部	(010)84254364
编 辑 部	(010)64210080
总 编 室	(010)64228516
网　　址	http://www.jccb.com.cn
电子邮箱	jinchengchuban@163.com
法律顾问	陈鹰律师事务所 (010)64970501

本书承蒙郭昌明基金资助印行

　　该基金以一位年近百岁的母亲的名字命名，她和中国近百年来一代又一代的普通母亲一样，将自己对人生和世界最美好的希望全部寄托给了成长中的中国式的世界公民。

The mission of the Center for Civic Education is to promote an enlightened, competent, and responsible citizenry. The curriculum materials prepared under this mandate are designed to advance this outcome. It is our goal to share these materials as widely as possible, to make them available to the students, teachers, and parents of the world, and not to limit distribution or to make profits for any individual.

美国公民教育中心以提高全体公民的文明程度、能力素养和责任感为己任，据此编写的课程教材，为达到这一结果而设计。我们的目标是尽可能广泛地分享这些课程教材，让世界上的学生、教师和家长都可以受用，不受限制地分发，也不为任何个人谋取利益。

All rights reserved. No part of this book may be reproduced or transmitted in any form or by any means, electronic or mechanical, or by any information storage and retrieval system, without permission in writing from the Center for Civic Education.

本书中文简体与英文对照版，由美国公民教育中心授权出版

未经公民教育中心书面许可，本书的任何部分都不得以任何形式或通过任何方式、电子方式或机械方式、或通过任何资料库和检索系统进行复制或者传播。

CENTER FOR CIVIC EDUCATION

5145 Douglas Fir Road

Calabasas, CA 91302 - USA

818.591.9321 - Fax 818.591.9330

cce@civiced.org

www.civiced.org

人类命运与责任共同体时代呼唤世界公民

——世界公民读本（文库）出版说明

刘建华

引子

早在大约 250 年前，中国与世界公民 (The Citizen of the World) 这个英文词组，就有过一次美丽的的邂逅。18 世纪 60 年代，中国在西方的许多思想家那里，被理想化为一个美好而神秘的国度，哥德斯密 (Oliver Goldsmith，1728—1774) 就是在这样的时代背景下，以"中国人的信札" (Chinese Letters) 为名，发表连载文章，借此讥讽英国的社会弊病，两年后（1763）结集出版，题名为：The Citizen of the World or Letters of a Chinese Philosopher living in London to his Friends in the East. 翻译成中文，是《世界公民—— 一位旅居伦敦的中国哲学家写给他的东方朋友的信札》。

此后过了约 150 年，大约距今 100 年前的 1914 年，一个在美国的中国人应验了歌德斯密的这个噱头式的玩笑。根据邵建先生发表在《大学人文》（广西师范大学出版社 2008 年 5 月版）的文章，这一年，在美国康奈尔大学的学生宿舍里，胡适在自己的一篇日记中，以《大同主义之先哲名言》为题，抄录了以下数则关于"世界公民"的先哲名言，这些名言以无言的方式，影响了无数个"胡适"们，并通过他们在后来的一个世纪里影响了无数中国人——

亚里斯提卜说过，智者的祖国就是世界。
——第欧根尼·拉尔修：《亚里斯提卜》第十三章

当有人问及他是何国之人时，第欧根尼回答道：

"我是世界之公民。"

　　——第欧根尼·拉尔修：《亚里斯提卜》第十三章

苏格拉底说，他既不是一个雅典人，也不是一个希腊人，

只不过是一个世界公民。

　　——普卢塔：《流放论》

我的祖国是世界，我的宗教是行善。

　　——T.潘恩：《人类的权利》第五章

世界是我的祖国，人类是我的同胞。

　　——W.L.加里森：《解放者简介》

一

　　进入 21 世纪以来，全球气候变暖的危机日益明显，与此相关的多种全球性危机日益增多，人类仿佛在一夜之间变得比以往任何时代都更加亲如兄弟、情同手足，地球比以往任何时候都更像是一个风雨飘摇中的小小的村落。这不只是全球经济一体化和信息技术与交通高度发达的结果，也不只是人类追求世界大同理想社会的结果，而是任何一个国家和民族都无法单独应对的全球共同的危机，让我们人类不得不彼此靠近，不能不唇齿相依，除了学会成为彼此一家的世界公民，学会互相之间兄弟姐妹般的友善和宽容，我们已经别无选择。

二

　　我们因此正在走向"人类命运共同体和全球责任共同体"的特殊时代，世界各国人民因此必须走出宗教文化壁垒，跨越意识形态障碍，超越政治制度边界，以世界公民的身份，与其他国家和民族的人民一道，共同承担起人类社会的可持续发展责任。我们每一个人不仅需要具有自觉的世界公民责任意识，更需要具有能承担起世界公民责任的基本素质和技能——在这样一个事关我们每一个人现在的生存质量、决定我们每一个家庭明天的

生活希望的全球性危机时代，我们每一个人都不能不从头开始，学会以世界公民的方式生存。

三

我们因此需要一个全球普遍适用的世界公民教育体系，但我们又身处多元格局的差异化社会之中，我们因此永远不可能有一部放之四海而皆准的世界公民统编教材，但是我们却可以而且必须互相参考和借鉴。我们因此倡导"互相阅读"和"比较阅读"式的世界公民教育，这本身就是一种承担共同责任的世界公民行为，是人类面对全球性危机时，首先需要的一种协商、协调、协同的智慧和行为。我们相信，尽管一方面，世界各国发展不平衡，世界各民族和地区的文化各不相同，应对全球性危机和承担世界公民责任的方式、方法和路径各不相同，但是，另一方面，世界各国无论贫富，世界各地无论远近，世界各民族文化无论有多么地不同，都毫无例外地、没有差别地、不可逃避地承受着同样的全球性危机的影响和压力，都必须协调一致，在人类的共同拯救行动中才能最终拯救自己。

四

综观世界各国的公民教育，无论是发达国家还是发展中国家，基本素质和基本技能都是公民教育的核心内容，唯其如此，世界各国的公民教育经验才具有互相参考和借鉴的可能性，不同语言的公民教育读本才具有互相阅读的必要性。

在众多国家出版的众多公民教育读本中，美国公民教育中心的一整套教材，在这方面最具有代表性。这套公民教育读本，可以说是"最高地位的社会名流邀请最高学问的专家一道，弯下腰来，以最低的姿态，奉献给他们认为是最高大的幼儿、少年、青年们的《公民圣经》"。这套由美国以及世界上多个国家多方面领域的专家经过多年精心编修的读本，没有高深的理论，没有刻板的道理，没有号称伟大的思想体系，没有不可置疑的绝对真理，而是结合人生成长的不同阶段，针对不同年龄青少年的学习、生活和成长实际，引导学生，通过自己的独立判断、反思鉴别、团队合作、谈判妥协、陈述坚持、提案答辩等理性的方法和智慧的工具，在观察、发现、认知、处理身边各种与公民权利和责任有关的问题的过程中，成长为一个具有公民美德基本素质和履行社会责任的基本技能的合格公民。

五

我们深知，无论多么好的公民素质和技能，离开了养成这种素质和技能的国度，就不一定有效，我们因此只是将这套美国公民教育读本作为中国公民的参考读物，原原本本地译介过来，用作借鉴，而非直接用作教材；我们深知，无论多么好的公民教育读本，离开了产生这种读本的文字语言环境，就很难领略其中丰富的意蕴，我们因此采用中英文对照的方式出版，即便是当作学习美国英语的泛读教材，也不失为一种明智的选择，因为这套读本用最基本的词汇和最浅显的文体，最准确地阐释了美国最基本的社会实质和美国公民最基本的生活真实。

六

《世界公民读本》（文库），是一项长期性的、庞大的公益出版计划，其宗旨在于倡导全社会的"公民阅读"。 公民阅读和私人兴趣阅读不一样的地方在于，私人阅读更关注个体自身的心灵世界、个人的知识需求和个性化的审美愉悦，而公民阅读更关心的是公共生活的领域、人类共同的价值和世界更好的未来。从这个意义上来说，公民阅读是一种更加需要精神品德和高尚情怀的开放式阅读、互动式阅读和参与式阅读，也正是在这个意义上，可以说，我们翻译出版给国人阅读的这套《世界公民读本》，其实也是真正意义上的《好人读本》、《成功读本》、《领袖读本》，是每一个人，要想成长、成熟、成功的基本教科书，是任何人一生中的"第一启蒙读本"。

七

我们的民族是一个崇尚"好人"的民族，深受"穷则独善其身，达则兼济天下"的自我完善文化影响，更有所谓"不在其位、不谋其政"的古老训条，这些都很容易被借用来为我们远离社会理想、逃避公民责任构建自我安慰的巢穴。人们因此更愿意以"独善"的"好人"自居，而怯于以"兼济"的"好公民"自励。

　　尽管我们的传统是一个没有公民的好人社会传统，但我们的时代却是一个需要好公民的大社会时代，在这样的文化纠结中，就让我们用世界公民的阅读方式延续中国的好人传统，用好人的传统善意理解当今的公民世界。这可以说是我们编辑出版《世界公民读本》（文库）的初衷。

八

　　我们期待着有一天，公民这个称呼，能够像"贤人"一样，成为令每一个中国人都值得骄傲的赞许；世界公民这个身份，能够像"圣人"一样，成为中华传统至高无上的美德的代名词。

　　我们相信有一天，一个普通的中国人面对世界的时候，也能够像美国的奥巴马一样，以世界公民的身份向世界的公民们说：

　　"Tonight, I speak to you not as a candidate for President, but as a citizen—a proud citizen of the United States, and a fellow citizen of the world."（今晚，我并不是以一个总统候选人的身份在这里向大家演讲，而是以一位公民——一位以美国为荣的公民和一位世界公民的身份跟大家讲话。）

　　"I am a citizen of the world."我是一个世界公民。你准备好了吗？

编者语

这是一些将民主与法治当作信仰，相信它能够成为社会的秩序原则与社会运行方式，并坚信理性力量的知识精英，历经数年共同精心编纂的一部书。他们满怀激情、充满智慧，以建筑一座理想中恢宏大厦的决心，做着构建最扎实地基的工作——公民教育。

被命名为《民主的基础》的这一辑的读者对象，是甫将开始独立社会生活的青年。这些青年，正是保证前人着力思考过、倾心建设过的民主与法治机制——同时也是具有普世价值的文化传统和社会生活信念，能够得以延续的基石。

作为美国高中的课程读本，《民主的基础》由《权威》、《隐私》、《责任》、《正义》四个部分构成。所涉问题常常会触碰到个体的自我面对群体的他者时的一些核心价值冲突，令我们本能、直觉的感受纠结与困扰。但是，我们都知道，这世界是由一个个独立的个体组成的一个共同体，社会共有的秩序与幸福是达成个体幸福的基础。在纷繁复杂的人际社会中、在相互冲突的利益与价值面前，必须权衡利弊，做出理性的思考与选择。因此，只有当一个社会有更多能够独立思考的人、以社会的共同利益为目标捍卫个人权利的人，我们才能够期待这个社会更加和谐美好。

该丛书的要旨不仅是带领研习者广泛而深入的思考权威、隐私、责任、正义这些至关重要的问题，更是通过思想智慧、知识经验给出了一个叫做"知识工具"的东西。"它是一种思想工具，是研究问题和制定决策的一系列思路与方法的集合。"运用这些工具，不仅能帮助我们更好地解析这些核心理念，更通过由理念到操作层面的分析与权衡，令研读者通过熟练运用具体的指标体系，形成对研究对象的判断与决策，在面对多重利益交叠的复杂的社会政治生活、决定我们的态度和行动方式的时候，超越情感，不是凭主观感受，而是理性、平和、有序的使用知识工具做出衡量与选择。

可以说，这套书是一部精粹的法治文化及公民教育领域的思想方法读本，是了解美国核心民主法治建构理念与公平公正处世方略的钥匙，是把握理性权衡与处置个体与社会共同体之间利益与冲突的工具，同时也是学习最简洁、规范、实用的文化英语和法律英语的范本。相信该丛书会从多个方面给予我们启迪。

Foundations of Democracy introduces you to four ideas which are basic to our constitutional form of government: authority, privacy, responsibility, and justice. These are not only ideas that need to be grasped in order to understand the foundations of our government, but they are crucial to evaluating the important differences between a constitutional democracy and a society that is not free.

《民主的基础》将向你们介绍美国政府的宪政模式中的四种基本观念：权威、隐私、责任和正义。理解和掌握这四种观念，不仅有助于理解美国政府的立国之本，更是评估和区分"宪政民主"与"不自由的社会"的关键。

Preface

Foundations of Democracy introduces you to four ideas which are basic to our constitutional form of government: authority, privacy, responsibility, and justice. These are not only ideas that need to be grasped in order to understand the foundations of our government, but they are crucial to evaluating the important differences between a constitutional democracy and a society that is not free.

There are costs or burdens that we must bear in order to preserve our freedom and the values on which our nation was founded. There are many situations in which hard choices need to be made between competing values and interests. In this course of study, you will be challenged to discuss and debate situations involving the use of authority and the protection of privacy. You will be asked to decide how responsibilities should be fulfilled and how justice could be achieved in a number of situations.

You will learn different approaches and ideas, which we call "intellectual tools," to evaluate these situations. Intellectual tools help you think clearly about issues of authority, privacy, responsibility, and justice. They help you develop your own positions, and support your positions which reasons.

The knowledge and skills you gain in this course of study will assist you not only in addressing issues of public policy, but also in everyday situations you face in your private life. By thinking for yourself, reaching your own conclusions, and defending your positions, you can be a more effective and active citizen in a free society.

前　言

　　《民主的基础》将向你们介绍美国政府的宪政模式中的四种基本观念：权威、隐私、责任和正义。理解和掌握这四种观念，不仅有助于理解美国政府的立国之本，更是评估和区分"宪政民主"与"不自由的社会"的关键。

　　为了维护我们的国家得以建立的自由和价值，我们必须付出代价或承担责任，我们也必须在许多相互冲突的价值和利益中做出选择。在本课程的学习中，你们将会针对运用权威和保护隐私的案例进行讨论和辩论，你们将要回答在一系列情况下应当如何承担责任、怎样才能实现正义的问题。

　　在本课程中，你们将学到各种不同的方法和观念（在这里我们统称为"知识工具"），并运用这些工具来评估不同的案例和情况。知识工具不仅将帮助你们对有关权威、隐私、责任和正义的问题进行更清晰的思考，也将有助于你们形成自己的观点，并通过推理来论证自己的观点。

　　在本课程学习过程中所获得的知识与技能，不仅将有助于你们应对未来的公共政策问题，也能帮助你们面对个人生活中的日常情况。通过独立思考，形成自己的观点并对此进行论证。作为一个公民的你，将更有效、更主动地投身于自由的社会中。

AUTHORITY
Table of Contents

目录

 What do Jefferson's words in the Declaration of Independence imply about the source of governmental authority?

关于政府权威的来源，杰斐逊在《独立宣言》中的这段话说明了什么？

Introduction

> "We hold these Truths to be self-evident...Govenments are instituted among Men, derivmg their just Powers from the Consent of the Governed ..."

This quotation from the Declaration of Independence contains one of our most basic ideas about government We, the people, give our government the authority to rule us. We give the government the right under certain conditions and limitations, to control our lives, liberty, and property.

We, as citizens, retain the ultimate fight to control how our government uses the authority we have delegated to it We exert this control by exercising our right to vote, by participating in the political process, and by having the government adhere to the limitations the Constitution imposes.

The rights of citizenship carry with them the responsibility to deal intelligently with issues of authority. To do this, we need to understand authority and make informed decisions about its use. We need to be able to answer such questions as "What is authority?" "Where does authority come from?" and "Why do we need authority?"

This text will help you gain a better understanding of the subject of authority and a greater ability to deal effectively with issues of authority as they arise in your life as a citizen in our free society.

导言

> "我们认为下面这些真理是不言而喻的…为了保障这些权利，人类才在他们之间建立政府，而政府之正当权力，是经被治理者的同意而产生的…"

这段摘自《独立宣言》的话包含了我们关于政府的最基本观念之一：我们，即人民，赋予了我们的政府以统治我们的权威。我们给了政府权利，在某种条件和限制下，去控制我们的生活、自由和财富。

我们，作为公民，保留着终极权利去控制我们的政府如何使用这些我们赋予它的权威。我们行使这种控制通过运用我们的权利去投票，通过参与到政治进程中，并通过使政府持续处于宪法的限制之下。

伴随着公民身份的权利而来的是需要智慧地处理权威的问题。为此，我们需要理解权威，并对它的使用做出明智的决定。我们需要能够回答类似的问题，例如"什么是权威？""权威来自何处？"以及"为什么我们需要权威？"

本文将帮助你对权威的主题有更好的理解，并使自由社会的公民之一的你在日常生活中遇到权威问题时能更好地有效地解决它们。

Unit One
What Is Authority?

> ### Purpose of Unit
>
> • When does someone have the right to tell you what to do?
> • When do you have the right to tell others what to do?

These are difficult questions. The answers have to do with authority-the rules and the people who govern our lives. We need to answer these questions to deal with issues of authority that confront us every day-at home, at school, in our jobs, and in our government.

In this unit you will begin to consider these questions. You will learn the difference between authority and power without authority-between those who have the right to use power and those who do not. You will examine different sources of authority and discuss the need for authority in society. This background will help you deal with difficult questions about people in authority and the rules that govern your life.

第一单元：什么是权威？

单元目标

· 人们什么时候有权利告诉你该做什么？

· 你什么时候有权利告诉他人该做什么？

这是两个不同的问题，答案与权威有关。在这里，权威是指那些支配我们生活的规则和人。我们需要回答这些问题以处理在日常生活中摆在我们面前的权威问题——不论是在家、在学校、在工作中和在我们的政府里。

在这一单元你们将开始考虑这些问题。你们将学会"权威"和"没有权威的权力"之间的区别——即那些有权利行使权力和无权的人之间的差别。你们将会研究权威的不同来源并讨论社会对权威的需求。这一背景知识将会帮助你们处理关于那些支配你的生活的处于权威地位的人和规则的棘手的问题。

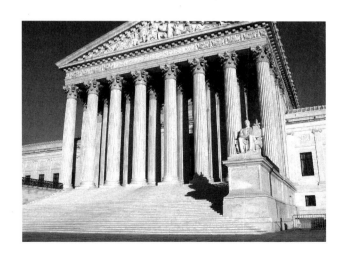

 How do these photographs illustrate authority?

这些照片如何表现了权威?

LESSON 1

What Is the Difference between Authority and Power Without Authority?

> ### Purpose of Lesson
>
> This lesson explains the definition of authority that we will use in this course of study. When you have completed this lesson, you should be able to explain the difference between authority and power without authority.

Terms to Know

authority	kangaroo court
power	paramilitary

Critical Thinking Exercise

DISTINGUISHING BETWEEN AUTHORITY AND POWER WITHOUT AUTHORITY

Read the news story below adapted from the July 6 1993 edition of The Wall Street Journal and then answer the 'What do you think" questions. Be prepared to share your answers with the class.

Vigilante Justice in Northern Ireland

By Tony Hurwitz Staff Reporter of THE WALL STREET JOURNAL

BELFAST, Northern Ireland -The knee cappers caught up with Eddie Kane outside a candy shop, in a Catholic/Protestant war zone known as "Murder Mile." Tossing a hood over his head, two masked men questioned Mr. Kane about an assault on one of their mates. Then they forced him to lie face down and pressed a gun to the back of his leg.

第一课   "权威"和"没有权威的权力"之间有什么区别?

本课目标

本课解释了我们在这门课程中将用到的"权威"的定义。学完本课后,你应当能够解释"权威"和"没有权威的权力"之间的区别。

掌握词汇

权威   私设法庭

权力   半军事化

重点思考练习

区别"权威"和"没有权威的权力"

阅读1993年7月6日的《华尔街日报》上摘录的新闻故事,并回答"你怎么看?"部分的问题。准备好与全班分享你的答案。

北爱尔兰的治安维持会的正义

撰稿:《华尔街日报》记者 托尼·霍维茨

北爱尔兰贝尔法斯特的天主教与新教冲突区之间一条叫做"谋杀之路"的糖果店外,两个蒙面的锁膝枪手绑架了埃迪·凯恩,把头罩蒙在他头上,并拷问他关于前不久发生的他们的伙伴遇袭事件。紧接着他们强迫凯恩脸朝下趴在地上,并对着他的腿后侧开了一枪。

"Kneecapping" in Northern Ireland dates back to the beginnings of the civil strife-known here as "the Troubles"-in 1969. At first an IRA (Irish Republican Army) punishment for informers, kneecapping has come to cover a range of alleged crimes.

There is a circular argument used to justify kneecapping. It goes as follows: The Troubles have caused citizens, Catholics in particular, to consider the police as enemies. Indeed, because paramilitary groups often ambush police, law-enforcement groups do have trouble combating ordinary crime. So, if someone steals your car, don't call the police (and risk being branded an informer). Call the "Provos"-the IRA-or, if you are a Protestant, call loyalist groups such as the Ulster Freedom Fighters, who will take action.

"Kneecapping is brutal, but what are you supposed to do?" Asks Maureen Mcguire, a Catholic mother of two sons, aged seven and eight Like many of her neighbors, she says "hoods" are running amok and police "won't or can't come get them."

Kneecapping has thus assumed the aura of a shadow legal system. People call it "rough justice," meted out by gunmen known as "circuit judges," who sometimes hold kangaroo courts. Defendants are found guilty of "antisocial behavior." Sentences are tailored to the misdeed. Minor miscreants pot-smokers, say-will be warned. On second offense they will be beaten or shot through the calf or thigh. More serious offenders get a bullet through the knee. If they don't reform, they are shot again, through several limbs.

Do you think the government of Nazi Germany exercised authority or power without authority? ☞

　　在北爱尔兰，这种用枪击穿膝盖的方法可以追溯到1969年的内乱（在北爱尔兰被人们称为"动乱"）初期。射膝最开始是爱尔兰共和军对告密者的一种惩罚，后来被用来对付许多其他所谓"罪行"。

　　证明射膝惩罚的正义性是一个恶性循环：动乱使北爱尔兰民众，特别是天主教徒，将警察视作敌人，而同时也因为这些半军事化团体经常伏击警察，使得法律执行人员很难打击普通犯罪。如果有人偷了你的车，千万别叫警察（这要冒着被打上告密者烙印的风险）；相反你应当给爱尔兰共和军打电话；或者如果你是一个新教徒，就应当联系当地反对独立的信仰团体，例如阿尔斯特自由战士，他们会为此采取行动。

　　"射膝的确很残忍，但换作是你，你该怎么办？" 一位天主教徒莫琳·麦克圭尔，同时也是两个7岁和8岁孩子的母亲问道。像她的很多邻居一样，她说"暴徒们"横行霸道，警察"不会来，也抓不到他们"。

　　射膝因而形成了一种"影子法律体系"的阴森气氛，人们把射膝枪手们叫做"巡回法官"，射膝被称作"粗暴的正义"，而枪手们负责执行这种正义。有的枪手也私设法庭，被告人因"反社会行为"而被起诉，法庭会针对其不当行为进行判决。轻微的罪行（例如吸大麻）会被警告。二次再犯，他们的小腿或大腿会被鞭打或枪击。更严重的罪犯会被射膝。如果仍不洗心革面，四肢还会再次被射。

你认为德国纳粹政府是在行使"权威"还是"没有权威的权力"？

"Crimes" now deemed to merit kneecapping include failure to pay dues to paramilitary groups.

While police in Belfast are indeed hampered by public distrust, by their fear of booby traps, and by the need to patrol inside armor-plated jeeps, constables hardly overlook common crime. In recent months police have arrested a number of those kneecapped as lawbreakers. Many are now awaiting trial in the local courts.

The police have also begun a program to investigate the knee cappers themselves for taking matters of law enforcement in their own hands and for conducting kangaroo courts.

The police have made a number of arrests and several former vigilantes await their day in a court of law.

What do you think?

1. Who in the news article is using power?

2. What is the difference between the use of power by paramilitary groups to punish suspected criminals and the use of power by government to punish suspected criminals through the court system?

3. How does the "shadow legal system" of kneecapping differ from an established legal system of police and courts? How is it similar to an established legal system?

Power or Authority?

The exercise you have just completed raises questions of power and authority. The distinction between the two ideas is important. You may have been in situations where someone used power to force you to do something against your will. Sometimes that person may have had the right to do so; other times he or she may not have had the right. When does someone have the right to control your behavior?

• Do your parents have the right to require you to be home at a certain time? Why or why not?

• Do you have the right to make your younger brother or sister leave the TV set alone? Why or why not?

现在，只要犯罪就会被射膝，罪行还包括没按时向这些半军事化团体缴纳会费。

出于对匪徒诱杀圈套的恐惧，贝尔法斯特警方不得不坐在装甲吉普车里巡逻，公众也因此无法信任警方。但普通犯罪仍然很难被忽略。最近几个月里，警察逮捕了许多违法的射膝枪手，当中有很多现在在地方法庭等待判决。

警方也开始着手调查射膝枪手亲自用武力强制执法和私设法庭的案件，逮捕了一些人，当中有许多曾经是"治安维持会"的成员，他们也将在一个合法的法庭上等待法律对自己的宣判。

你怎么看？

1. 在这篇新闻报道中，谁正在运用权力？
2. 这些半军事化团体惩罚嫌犯时所运用的权力，和政府通过法律体系惩罚嫌犯所运用的权力之间有什么不同？
3. 射膝枪手的"影子法律体系"，与现有的警察和法院组成的法律体系之间有什么不同？有什么相同？

权力还是权威？

上个练习中提出了关于权力和权威的问题。区分这两种概念是很重要的。你也许曾经遭遇过某些人使用权力迫使你做某些违背你意愿的事的情况。有时候那个人可能有"权利"那么做，有时候他或她可能并没有这种"权利"。什么时候某些人可以有权控制你的行为？

- 你的父母是否有权利要求你在某个规定的时间内回家？

　为什么有？为什么没有？

- 你是否有权利让你的弟弟或妹妹把电视让给你看？

　为什么有？为什么没有？

- Does your principal have the right to require you not to leave the school campus during the school day? Why or why not?
- Does your friend have the right to force you to do something you do not want to do? Why or why not?
- Does the government have the right to require you to obey a law that you believe is wrong? Why or why not?

To answer these questions, we need to know the difference between power and authority. Although there may be more than one way to define these terms, for our purposes we will use the following definitions:

- **Power** is the ability to control or direct something or someone. Sometimes people have the right to use power; sometimes they do not.
- When a thief robs you at gunpoint, he has the power to do so. He does not have the right.
- When the Supreme Court says a law is unconstitutional, it has both the power and the right to do so.

How do justices of the U.S. Supreme Court acquire both power and authority to declare laws unconstitutional? ☞

- 你的校长是否有权利要求你在上课时间不许离开学校？

  为什么有？为什么没有？

- 你的朋友是否有权利要求你做某些你不想做的事情？

  为什么有？为什么没有？

- 政府是否有权利要求你遵守某项你认为是错误的法律？

  为什么有？为什么没有？

要回答这些问题，我们需要了解权力和权威之间的不同。尽管有许多方法定义这些词汇，在本课中，我们将运用以下定义：

权力：是一种控制或指挥某事或某人的能力。有时人们有行使权力的权利，有时没有。

- 当一个窃贼持枪抢劫你时，他有权力让你按照他的要求去做，但他没有权利这么做。

- 当最高法院判定某项法律是违宪的，它有权力也有权利这样判定。

美国最高法院的法官们如何获得了判定法律是否合宪的权力和权威？

- **Authority** is power combined with the right to use that power. The right to use power usually comes from laws, customs, or principles of morality.
- Police officers have the authority to arrest a person because the law gives them that right.
- Congress has the authority to pass a law because the Constitution gives it that right.

Critical Thinking Exercise

DESCRIBING THE DIFFERENCE BETWEEN AUTHORITY AND POWER WITHOUT AUTHORITY

To help you understand the difference between authority and power without authority, read the sentences below and answer the questions that follow. Be prepared to explain your answers to the class.

1. Police officer Karen Weidman gives Allison Green a ticket for speeding.

2. Jerry Robinson tells Marty Karinsky to stay away from his girlfriend or Jerry will "take care of him."

3. Judge Alvarez places Maggie Jones on probation.

4. The government imprisons Juan Rodriguez for refusing to serve in the army during the Vietnam war because of his belief that it is morally wrong to kill.

Do you think the government should have had the authority to arrest those who burned their draft cards to protest the Vietnam war? ☞

权威：是一种权力，并伴随着可以行使这种权力的权利。这种行使权力的权利通常来源于法律、习俗或道德准则。

- 警察有权威逮捕一个人，因为法律赋予了他们这样的权利；
- 国会有权威通过一项法律，因为宪法赋予了它这样的权利。

重点思考练习

描述"权威"以及"没有权威的权力"

为了帮助你们理解权威和缺乏权威的权力之间的区别，阅读以下句子，并回答问题。准备好向全班解释你的答案。

1. 警察卡伦・韦德曼给阿利森・格林开了一张超速的罚单。
2. 杰利・鲁宾逊让马蒂　卡林斯基离他的女朋友远点儿，否则他会"好好照顾"马蒂。
3. 法官阿尔瓦・雷斯判处玛吉・琼斯缓刑。
4. 由于胡安・罗德里格拒绝在越南战争期间服兵役，政府将他关进监狱，而胡安的理由是，在他的宗教信仰里杀戮是不道德的。

你认为政府是否应当有权威逮捕那些烧掉自己的征兵卡以抗议越南战争的人？

5. Arturo Lopez tells his daughter that she will have to stay home all week because she was out past her curfew on Saturday night.

6. Bob Jackson, who is bigger than most of his classmates, cuts in front of the cafeteria line.

7. Jane Doe, the owner of an illegal gambling house, tells a customer to pay his debt or prepare for trouble.

8. Two members of a gang shoot and cripple Eddie Kane for revenge.

9. Ali Darwish tells the two girls sitting next to him in the movie theater to move because they are making too much noise.

10. The manager tells Sally Hu that she is not allowed to smoke in the "no smoking" section of the restaurant.

What do you think?

1. Which situations illustrate the use of authority? Why?

2. Which situations illustrate the use of power without authority? Why?

3. Why is it important to know the difference between authority and power without authority?

Using the Lesson

1. While you are studying Authority, you should keep a journal. Begin by writing brief descriptions of four real or imaginary incidents that illustrate the use of authority and the use of power without authority. Make two of the descriptions examples of authority and the other two examples of power without authority. You may use incidents from your experiences or from newspapers, magazines, books, television, or movies.

2. Bring two news clippings to class that illustrate the use of authority or power without authority and explain them.

5. 阿特诺·洛佩兹告诉他的女儿，她必须整个星期都呆在家里，因为上
   周六晚，她超过了门禁时间回家。

6. 在自助餐厅排队吃饭时，鲍勃·杰克逊常常因为自己是班上年龄最大
   的而插队。

7. 简·多伊开了一家非法的赌博店，她警告她的客人必须还帐，否则就
   等着麻烦上门。

8. 一个流氓团伙的两名成员出于报复而枪击了爱迪·凯恩并致其残疾。

9. 在电影院里，阿里·达尔维什让坐在他旁边的两个女孩走开，因为她
   们太吵了。

10. 餐厅经理跟萨利·胡说，她不可以在餐厅的"禁烟区"吸烟。

你怎么看?

1. 以上哪一种情况运用了"权威"？为什么？

2. 以上哪一种情况运用了"没有权威的权力"？为什么？

3. 为什么有必要了解"权威"和"没有权威的权力"之间的区别？

知识运用

1. 当你们在学习"权威"部分的时候，应当记一本笔记。先简单地用
   四个真实的或想象的事例来描述运用了"权威"和"没有权威的权
   力"的不同情况，分别用两个事例描述"权威"的运用，再用两个
   来描述运用"没有权威的权力"的情况。可以从自己的经历中寻找
   事例，也可以从报纸、杂志、书本、电视或电影里寻找。

2. 带两篇新闻剪报来学校，向全班说明"权威"或"没有权威的权
   力"的运用，并阐述你所选用的材料。

LESSON 2

What Are Some Sources of Authority?

Purpose of Lesson

In this lesson you will learn where to find authority and some common arguments made to justify authority. When you have finished the lesson, you should be able to identify examples of authority and explain different arguments about its sources and justification.

Terms to Know

roles	divine right
institutions	consent
supreme being	source of authority
monarchies	aristocracies

Where can you find authority?

Where can you find authority? Every day we can see examples of people who have the authority to govern us and how we act. Parents, teachers, police officers, and government officials are just some of the people who have the authority to control our actions. Rules and laws also control or influence our behavior. Some of the most common places we can find authority include the following:

• **Rules and Laws.** Rules and laws control people's behavior. In this sense, they have authority. For example, when you obey a law requiring you to attend school, you are recognizing the authority of that law.

第二课：权威有哪些来源?

> ### 本课目标
>
> 　　在这一课中你们将会学习如何找到权威，以及如何找到用来证明权威正当性的常用论据。学完本课后，你们应当能够在案例中找出权威，并能解释各种有关权威来源和依据的不同观点。

掌握词汇

职能	神授的权利
机构	同意
至高无上之神	权威来源
君主	贵族

在哪里可以找到权威?

在哪里可以找到权威？每天我们都能遇到那些有权威支配我们并教我们如何行事的人。父母、老师、警察和政府官员都是这样一些有权威控制我们的行动的人。规则和法律也控制或影响着我们的行为。以下就是我们通常会遇到的权威：

- **规则和法律**：规则和法律控制着人们的行为，这意味着它们拥有权威。例如：因为遵守某项法律，你必须要去学校上学，这就表示你承认这项法律的权威。

- **Customs.** Customs are ways of behavior that people have engaged in for a long time. When customs control people's behavior, they may be said to have authority. For example, when you follow the practice of "first come, first served," you are recognizing the authority of a well-established custom.

- **Roles.** Certain roles carry with them the right to control people, no matter who fills these roles. For example, anyone filling the role of a police officer has the authority to require people to obey traffic laws.

- **Institutions.** Groups of people working together in certain institutions also have the authority to control or influence others. For example, Congress as an institution, and not its individual members, has the authority to pass laws that people must obey.

- **Principles of Morality.** Fundamental ideas about right and wrong that come from religion, ethics, and individual conscience often govern our behavior. For example, the Bible has authority for many people.

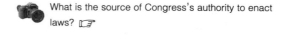

What is the source of Congress's authority to enact laws? ☞

- **习俗**：习俗是人们长期形成的行为方式。当习俗控制着人们的行为时，它们就被认为是具有权威的。例如：当你遵循"先到先得"的习俗行事时，你就是在认可这项固有习俗的权威。
- **职能**：某些职能本身具有控制他人的权利，无论是谁担任了这项职务都是如此。例如：不管是谁担任了警察的工作，他就有权威要求人们遵守交通法规。
- **机构**：在某些机构中共同工作的一群人，同时也拥有控制或影响他人的权利。例如：国会作为一个机构（而非个体成员），有权利批准某项法律，并要求人们必须遵守这些法律。
- **道德准则**：来自宗教、伦理和个人良知的一些基本的是非观念，通常支配着我们的行动。例如，圣经对许多人来说具有权威。

国会制定法律的权威来源是什么？

Where does authority come from?

We have seen that authority may be found in a number of places, but where does it come from? How do certain roles, institutions, laws, customs, and moral principles get the authority, or right, to control our behavior? Where does the police officer get the right to tell us what to do? Why do some people believe that the Bible has the authority to govern their actions? Where does Congress get the right to pass laws we must obey? In short, what is the source of authority?

Sometimes the source of authority for a rule or a position may be traced back through a number of steps. For example: the authority of a teacher to maintain order in the class can be traced back to the principal in charge of the school, who hired the teacher, to the superintendent who appointed the principal, and to the board of education that appointed the superintendent. From here it can be traced back to the state board of education, and to the laws that gave it the authority to make regulations about how schools should be run. Finally, authority can be traced to the state legislature that made the laws, and to the state constitution that established the state legislature.

Eventually, however, we can ask, "What is the ultimate or final source of authority for government? For customs? For moral principles?" Depending on the answers, we may conclude that claims to authority are justified or unjustified. That is, examining the source of authority for a government, a custom, or a moral principle can help us decide whether we ought to obey it. For example: the ultimate authority of some customs may be simply that they have been followed for so long they are accepted without thought. If these customs are not supported by any good reason, you might decide not to follow them.

What arguments are made to justify the authority of rulers and governments?

Historically, rulers or governments have claimed their authority from one or more of the following sources:

权威从哪儿来？

我们已经知道权威可能出现在许多地方，但它到底从哪儿来？那些职能、机构、法律、习俗和道德准则又是怎样获得了权威、或拥有权利控制我们的行为呢？警察告诉我们应当做什么的权利是从何而来的？为什么有些人相信圣经有控制他们行动的权威？国会又是从哪里获得了批准法律并让我们必须遵守的权利呢？简而言之，权威的来源是什么？

有时候，我们可以通过一系列步骤来追溯某项规则或某个职位的权威来源。例如：一个老师在课堂上维持秩序的权威可以追溯到聘用这位老师并管理学校的校长、追溯到任命校长的教育局长、追溯到任命教育局长的教育委员会。从这里我们可以看出权威来源于教育委员会，以及来自于某些法律，正是这些法律赋予了委员会以制定学校管理规章的权威。最终，老师的权威可以归结为制定法律的国家立法机构，以及建立立法机构的国家宪法。

那么我们可能会接着问："政府权威的最根本的或最终的来源是什么？习俗的来源呢？道德准则的呢？"根据来源的不同，我们可以判断这些权威是合理的或不合理的。也就是说，找出一个政府、一项习俗或一种道德准则的权威来源，可以帮助我们判断是否应当服从它们的权威。例如：某些习俗的最终权威来源，可能仅仅只是因为长久以来人们不假思索地接受并追随了这样的习俗。如果这些习俗没有任何充分的理由支持，你可以决定不去遵守它们。

什么样的论据是用来证明统治者和政府的权威的？

历史上，统治者或政府曾经声称他们的权威来源于以下一种或多种来源：

- **Birth.** Some rulers have said that they inherited their authority from earlier rulers who received their right to govern from a Supreme Being. Hereditary monarchies and aristocracies have made such claims.

- **Knowledge.** Some people have claimed that those with superior knowledge should have the right to rule.

- **Consent of the Governed.** Many governments today claim that their authority comes from the people who are the ultimate source of authority. The people give their consent to the government and agree to be ruled by it.

- **A Supreme Being.** Rulers have often claimed that their authority comes from a Supreme Being or God. For example, kings and queens have often said they rule by divine right; that is, they get their authority from God.

 How do the words in the Pledge of Allegiance reflect the idea of consent of the governed as a source of government authority? In what other ways do people exhibit their consent to be ruled by the government? ☞

- **出身**：某些统治者声称自己继承了前任统治者的权威，而他们的前任获得统治的权利是从一种至高无上的神而来。世袭的君主和贵族都曾经提出过这样的观点。
- **知识**：某些人声称那些拥有出众学识的人应当有统治的权利。
- **被统治者的同意**：当今许多政府声称他们的权力来自人民，并认为这是权威的终极来源。人民给予政府认可，并同意由政府来进行治理。
- **至高无上的神明**：统治者们也常常声称他们的权威来自某个至高无上的神，或上帝。例如，无论是国王还是女王，都通常说他们的统治是一种神圣权利，即，他们从上帝手中得到了权威。

宣誓效忠的誓词，是如何体现出"被统治者的同意是政府权威的来源之一"这种观念的？人们表现和表达自己对政府权威的同意还有什么别的方式吗？

Why is it important to know the source of authority?

We need to know the source of people's authority to determine if they have the right to do what they are doing. If we know, for example, that the Constitution gives certain powers to Congress, we can look at the Constitution to judge whether or not a law passed by Congress is within the limits of its authority. We can also ask for the source of the Constitution's authority. In our democratic form of government, the authority of the Constitution comes from the consent of the people.

People have different ideas about what should be considered to be a source of authority. They also may differ on which sources of authority should be considered more important or higher than others. To discuss such questions, it is necessary to identify and evaluate different sources of authority.

Critical Thinking Exercise

IDENTIFYING SOURCES OF AUTHORITY

Each of the following selections deals with a different source of authority. Your teacher will divide your class into five groups to complete this exercise. Each group should read the selection assigned to it, discuss the questions that follow, and choose a spokesperson to report the group's answers to the class.

Group 1: The Law of Hospitality

This selection is adapted from The Story of the Rheingold, a folk tale from German and Scandinavian literature. It explains why the hero, Siegmund, could feel safe spending the night at the castle of his sworn enemy, Hunding.

There were three reasons why Siegmund had to spend the night in Hunding's castle. First, Siegmund was too brave a hero to fly from danger. Second, Siegmund did not want to leave the beautiful maiden alone with Hunding, the cruel and evil robber. Third, Hunding had said, "Custom makes you safe as a guest in my house." This meant that it would be unfair and wrong for Hunding to harm Siegmund while he was taking shelter under Hunding's roof. This was called the Law of Hospitality. Just as no host ever harmed a guest, no honorable guest ever took advantage of the law.

为什么了解权威的来源是重要的?

我们需要首先了解人们权威的来源,才能判断掌握权威的人是否有权利做那些事。例如:如果我们知道是宪法赋予了国会某些权力,我们就能依据宪法来判断国会通过的某项法律是否超出了它的权威范围。我们也可以追问:宪法权威的来源是什么?在我们美国的民主政府体制中,宪法的权威来自于人民的同意。

对于权威的来源应当有哪些,人们各有不同想法。在权威的来源当中,某一种权威来源是否比其他来源更重要或地位更高,人们也会有不同看法。要讨论这些问题,就必须先识别和评估不同的权威来源。

重点思考练习

找出权威的来源

以下每组文摘都针对某一种独特的权威来源。老师将会把你们班分成五组来完成本练习,并为每一组指定阅读一段文字材料。讨论每段材料后的问题,每组选派一位代表发言,向全班汇报自己小组的答案。

第一组:待客之道

(悦纳异己法则The Law of Hospitality)

以下材料节选自《瑞恩高德的故事》(德国和斯堪的纳维亚文学中的一个民间故事)。它讲述了大英雄齐格蒙德为什么能在他不共戴天的仇敌洪丁的城堡中安全过夜的故事。

齐格蒙德必须在洪丁的城堡中过夜有三个原因:首先,齐格蒙德是一个非常勇敢的英雄,所以他无法逃避危险;其次,齐格蒙德不想让美丽的少女单独留在洪丁这个残酷、邪恶的强盗身边;第三,洪丁曾说过:"按照约定俗成的惯例,作为我的客人,你在我的家里很安全"。这意味着,只要齐格蒙德身处洪丁家的屋檐下,任何伤害齐格蒙德的举动都是不公平和错误的。这被称为"待客之道(悦纳异己法则 The Law of Hospitality)"。正如没有任何一位主人会伤害客人一样,同样地,任何一位尊贵的客人也不会利用这一规则伤害主人。

If Siegmund had run away in the night with the maiden, after Hunding had so well observed the Law of Hospitality, he would have been dishonorable as well as cowardly. It was just as though Siegmund had given a promise to Hunding that he would not go away that night.

What do you think?

1. What is a custom?

2. How can a custom be a source of authority?

3. What are other examples of authority that have their source in custom or tradition?

4. What are some advantages and disadvantages of being bound by custom?

Group 2: Tinker v. Des Moines Independent School District (1969)

In December 1965, a small group of students and their parents in Des Moines, Iowa, decided to express their opposition to the Vietnam War by wearing black armbands. The principals of the public schools heard of the plan and adopted a policy specifically prohibiting students from wearing black armbands and peace symbols in school. The Tinker children knew of the school policy and understood they would be suspended if they disobeyed the rule. On December 16 and 17, they wore black armbands to school. No disruptions of classroom activities, no demonstrations, and no threats of violence occurred.

 What might the Tinker children claim as the source of their authority for wearing black armbands to school? ☞

如果洪丁很好地遵守了"待客之道（悦纳异己法则 The Law of Hospitality）"，那么正如齐格蒙德答应自己当晚不会逃走一样，若是最后齐格蒙德带着少女逃跑了，英雄就会变成可耻的胆小鬼。

你怎么看？

1. 什么是习俗？
2. 习俗如何变成一种权威的来源？
3. 你们还能列举出其他来源于习俗或传统的权威的例子吗？
4. 被习俗约束有哪些优势和劣势？

第二组：1969年廷克诉德梅因独立学区案

1965 年 12 月，爱荷华州德梅因市的几名学生和他们的父母决定通过佩戴黑色袖章来表达对越南战争的反对。当地一所公立学校的校长听说了这件事，便采取了一项措施：明确禁止学生们在学校佩戴黑色袖章与和平标志。廷克家的孩子们听说了学校的政策，他们也知道如果违反了学校的规定他们将会被停学。12 月 16 日和 17 日，廷克家的孩子们还是戴着黑色的袖章到了学校，期间学校并没有发生任何课堂活动中断的状况，也没有发生任何示威和暴力威胁事件。

廷克家的孩子可以用什么作为他们在学校佩戴黑色袖章的权威来源？

The principal of the school that the Tinkers attended called the students into his office and asked them to remove the armbands. They refused and were suspended until they agreed to attend school without the armbands. Mr. Tinker filed a complaint on behalf of his children claiming that the school had violated their right to free expression. He said that the children had not interfered with the rights of other students nor had they disrupted class routine. The school officials argued that they had made the ruling to avoid a disruption of school discipline. Schools, they claimed, were no place for political demonstrations.

The Supreme Court eventually heard the case and ruled in the students' favor. The Court claimed that the wearing of armbands was a form of expression that was protected under the First Amendment. In the majority opinion the Court stated, "It can hardly be argued that either students or teachers shed their constitutional rights to freedom of speech or expression at the schoolhouse gate."

What do you think?

1. What was the source of authority for the school's policy on wearing armbands?

2. What was the source of authority for the Supreme Court's decision?

3. What is the source of authority for the Constitution?

4. What are some advantages and disadvantages of being bound by the Constitution?

Group 3: "On the Duty of Civil Disobedience"

The selection below is adapted from an essay by the American essayist, Henry David Thoreau (1817-1862). Thoreau chose not to pay his poll tax as a form of protest against slavery and the war with Mexico. Authorities arrested him and he spent a night in jail. A few years later in 1849, he wrote the now classic defense of individual conscience, "On the Duty of Civil Disobedience."

校长把廷克家的孩子们叫到自己的办公室，并要求他们摘掉袖章。孩子们拒绝了，随即便被学校要求停学，直到同意不戴袖章才能继续上学。随后，廷克先生以他的孩子们的名义提起了上诉。廷克先生认为，学校侵犯了孩子们自由表达的权利。他认为自己的孩子并没有干预其他学生的权利，也没有扰乱课堂秩序。而学校的官员们则认为，学校已经明确制定了规则以避免学生破坏学校纪律的行为。同时他们也认为，学校不是政治示威的场所。

最高法院最终聆讯了此案，并判学生们获胜。法院认为，佩戴袖章是一种表达形式，受第一宪法修正案的保护。法院的主要观点是："无论学生还是老师，在学校门口行使宪法关于言论和表达自由的权利，都是无可厚非的。"

你怎么看?

1. 学校规定禁止佩戴袖章的权威来源是什么?
2. 最高法院裁决的权威来源是什么?
3. 宪法权威的来源是什么?
4. 被宪法约束有哪些优势和劣势?

第三组：《论公民的不服从权利》

以下段落改编自美国作家亨利·戴维·梭罗（1817-1862）的一篇文章。作为自己反对黑奴制和美国与墨西哥战争的一种形式,梭罗因拒绝支付"人头税"而被当局逮捕入狱，一天后被释放。几年后的 1849 年，他写下了如今非常著名的有关个人良知的经典辩词——《论公民的不服从权利》。

Must the citizen ever give up his or her conscience to the legislator? Why does every person have a conscience then? I think we should be human beings first and subjects afterward. It is not desirable to cultivate a respect for the law so much as a respect for what is right. The only obligation I have is to do what is right. Law never made people act justly. In fact, many people who respect the law act unjustly because of it. A common and natural result of an undue respect for law is the following example: you have a line of soldiers colonel, captain, corporal, privates-all marching in order over hill and dale to wars that are against their common sense and conscience. They have no doubt that the wars are wrong. They are all peacefully inclined. Now, what are they-people or small moveable forts and guns at the service of those in power?

What do you think?

1. What sources of authority does Thoreau write about?

2. How can individual conscience or a personal sense of morality be a source of authority?

3. Is there a higher law than that of the government? Why or why not?

4. When, if ever, should a person refuse to obey a law he or she thinks is unjust?

What did Henry David Thoreau claim as the source of authority for his protest against the Mexican–American War of 1846? ☞

　　"公民是否必须在任何时候、或在最小程度上都使他的良心屈从于法律呢？那么，为何每人都有良知呢？我想，我们首先应该是人，然后才是国民。培养对法律的尊重，就像尊重正义一样，是令人不快的。我唯一应当承担的义务，是做我认为正当的事。法律绝不会使人做出正义的举动。实际上，许多尊重法律的人却因此变成不正义的行动者。对法律的过度尊重，其常见而自然的结果之一就是，你可以看见一队上校、上尉、下士、列兵等等，井然有序地列队翻山越岭，行进出征，违背他们的常识与良心。他们毫不怀疑，这场战争是错误的，他们都倾向和平。现在，他们是什么？是人？还是一些为那些掌权者服务的小型移动堡垒和弹药库？"

你怎么看？

1. 梭罗所描述的权威的来源是什么？
2. 个人的良知或个人的道德感如何能成为一种权力的来源？
3. 是否有一种法律高于政府的法律？为什么有？为什么没有？
4. 个人应当在何时（如果有的话）拒绝服从一种他或她认为不正义的法律？

亨利•戴维•梭罗用什么来作为他反对1846年美西战争的权威来源？

Group 4: The Mayflower Compact

The wind carried the Mayflower and its passengers to a place in the New World that was further north than they intended. Finding themselves outside the jurisdiction of their original charter from the Virginia Company, the Pilgrims decided to create their own government. In November 1620, they drew up an agreement that the forty-one men aboard the ship signed. By the terms of this agreement, known as the Mayflower Compact, the Pilgrims agreed to govern themselves.

In the Mayflower Compact, the Pilgrims decided, "there should be an agreement that we should combine together in: one body, and submit to such government, and governors as we should by common consent agree to make and choose." They agreed that it was best "to combine together into a civil body politic" that would create laws, constitutions, acts, and offices that were thought to be for the general good of the colony. The Pilgrims agreed to follow and obey this authority that they had created by their mutual consent.

The Mayflower Compact remained in force from 1620 until 1691, when the colony at Plymouth became part of the Massachusetts Bay Colony.

 What source of authority might the govemor of Plymouth Colony claim under the Mayflower Compact? ☞

第四组：《五月花号公约》

　　"五月花号"和它的乘客们被风吹着到达了新大陆，这是比他们的预定目的地更北边的地方。他们发现这里处于出发前与弗吉尼亚公司签订的条约管辖范围之外。因此，他们决定创立自己的政府。1620年11月，"五月花号"船上的41位男乘客起草并签署了一份名为《五月花号公约》的协议，并一致同意依照该协议进行自治。

　　在《五月花号公约》中，清教徒们决议："我们应当结合在一起，订立一项协议：作为一个整体，服从于我们一致同意而建立起来的政府和选择出来的统治者。"他们一致认为，最好是"团结在一起，成为一个民间政治团体"，制定符合殖民地公共利益的法律、宪法、法令和办事机构。这些清教徒一致同意遵循和服从这种根据"一致同意"建立的权威。

　　《五月花号公约》从1620年生效直至1691年普利茅斯殖民地并入马萨诸塞湾殖民地为止，一直发挥着它的权威效力。

《五月花号公约》之下，普利茅斯政府可以要求怎样的权威来源？

What do you think?

1. What was the source of the authority of the Mayflower Compact?

2. What was the belief underlying the Mayflower Compact about the source of a government's authority to make laws?

3. If some on board the ship had refused to sign, would they have been bound to obey it?

4. Since the men did not ask the women to sign the Compact, were they bound by its authority? Were children? Why or why not?

Group 5: The Constitution of the United States

The Constitution of the United States was drafted in Philadelphia in 1787. It did not become effective until the states ratified it. The following excerpts from the Constitution identify the source of the federal government's authority.

Preamble

We the People of the United States, in Order to form a more perfect Union, establish justice, insure domestic tranquillity, provide for the common defence, promote the general Welfare, and secure the Blessings of Liberty to ourselves and our Posterity, do ordain and establish this Constitution for the United States of America.

What source of authority might the Framers claim for the Constitution of the United States? ☞

你怎么看?

1. 《五月花号公约》的权威来源是什么?

2. 《五月花号公约》中所涉及的"政府制定法律的权威来源"体现了什么信仰?

3. 如果船上有人拒绝签署该公约,他们必须要遵守公约内容吗?

4. 船上的妇女们并没有签署这项公约,她们会受它的权威约束吗?那么儿童呢?为什么?为什么不?

第五组:美国宪法

　　美国宪法起草于1787年的费城,直到各州批准后才开始正式生效。以下宪法摘录明确了美国联邦政府权威的来源。

序言

　　"我们美利坚合众国的人民,为了组织一个更完善的联邦,树立正义,保障国内的安宁,建立共同的国防,增进全民福利和确保我们自己及我们后代能安享自由带来的幸福,乃为美利坚合众国制定和确立这一部宪法。"

对美国宪法的制订者们来说,他们可能要求的权威来源是什么?

Article I

Section 1. All legislative Powers herein granted shall be vested in a Congress of the United States, which shall consist of a Senate and a House of Representatives.

Article II

Section 1. The executive Power shall be vested in a President of the United States of America.

Article III

Section 1. The judicial Power of the United States shall be vested in one supreme Court, and in such inferior Courts as the Congress may from time to time ordain and establish.

What do you think?

1. What is the source of authority for the Constitution?

2. What is the source of authority for the Congress? For the president? For the Supreme Court?

3. What beliefs about the source of authority of government underlie the Constitution? Do you think these beliefs are justified? Why or why not?

Using the Lesson

1. In your journal briefly describe three situations from your experience in which you exercised authority that came from different sources.

2. Consider the authority of a police officer who gives someone a ticket for speeding. Draw a chart or illustration that traces the authority of the officer back to its ultimate source. Be prepared to explain your chart to the class.

3. Write an editorial either opposing or defending the position of the Tinker children. Describe the source of authority for their actions.

第一条

第一款：本宪法所规定的立法权，全属合众国的国会，国会由一个参议院和一个众议院组成。

第二条

第一款：行政权力赋予美利坚合众国总统。

第三条

第一款：合众国的司法权属于一个最高法院以及由国会随时下令设立的低级法院。

你怎么看?

1. 宪法的权威来源是什么？
2. 国会的权威来源是什么？总统的呢？最高法院的呢？
3. 宪法中体现了有关政府权威来源的什么信仰？你认为这些信仰是否合理？为什么？为什么不？

知识运用

1. 在你的笔记中描述三种状况，选取你自己行使不同来源的权威的经验。

2. 想想一位给司机开超速罚单的警官的权威，追溯这位警官的权威直至最终源头，画一幅图表或图示来说明，并准备向全班同学解释你的图示。

3. 写一篇评论，或反对、或支持廷克先生的观点，并描述他们行为的权威来源。

LESSON 3
How Can We Use Authority?

Purpose of Lesson

In this lesson you will learn some uses of authority. You will examine two views on the need for governmental authority and evaluate a situation in which government authority helped to resolve a dispute about water pollution. When you have completed this lesson you should be able to explain how authority can be used to deal with problems.

Term to Know

state of nature

Why do we need authority?

Think of all the rules you follow every day. Then think about all the people in authority who sometimes tell you what to do. Are there too many rules? Are there too many people in authority?

 How do the 1992 Los Angeles riots illustrate the need for authority? ☞

第三课：如何运用权威？

本课目标

在本课中，你们将会学到某些权威的运用，并研究两种有关政府权威的需求的观点，并要评估政府权威帮助解决水污染纠纷的情况。学完本课后，你们应当能解释权威是如何用来解决问题的。

掌握词汇

自然状态

为什么我们需要权威？

想想你每天所遵守的规则。然后再想想那些时常告诉你应该怎么做的有权威的人。规则会不会太多？有权威的人是不是也太多？

1992年洛杉矶暴动如何体现了对权威的需求？

Have you ever wondered what might happen if there were no rules and no people in authority? Imagine that you wake up one morning and all rules, laws, police, courts, school administrators, and governments have disappeared.

• What problems might arise?

• Would you have any rights?

• How would you protect your rights?

Critical Thinking Exercise

EVALUATING AND TAKING A POSITION ON THE NECESSITY OF GOVERNMENT

Read the two essays on the next page. Then with a study partner discuss the questions in the "What do you think?" section. Be prepared to share your answers with the class.

Adapted from "Two Treatises of Civil Government" John Locke (1690)

Many people have thought about what life would be like without government, rules, and laws. John Locke (1632-1704), an English philosopher, wrote about life in a state of nature, an imaginary condition in which people lived together without government.

People are free in the state of nature. Why do they give up this freedom and subject themselves to the authority of government? The answer to this question is obvious: in the state of nature the enjoyment of freedom is very uncertain. People are always open to attacks from others. Life is dangerous and full of fear. That is why people seek others who share their need for security and join with them. They do so in an effort to protect their lives, their liberty, and their property.

In the state of nature there are many things missing to maintain a secure life. First, there is no established system of law that all people have agreed on and which all people know. And since there is no law, there is no standard of right and wrong that people can use to settle disagreements between them. Second, there is no judge with the authority to settle arguments. Third, there is no person or group of people who have the authority to enforce the law.

你有没有想过，如果不存在有权威的规则和人，将会发生什么？假设某天早晨你醒来时发现所有的规则、法律、警察、法院、学校管理者和政府都消失了：

- 可能会出现什么问题？
- 你将会有什么权利？
- 你将如何保护自己的权利？

重点思考练习

评估政府的必要性并表明你的观点

阅读以下两篇文章，然后与一位同学合作讨论"你怎么看？"部分的问题。准备与全班同学分享你们的答案。

摘自：《政府论》

作者：约翰·洛克 （1690年）

许多人曾经想过如果没有政府、规则和法律，生活会变成怎样。 一位英国哲学家约翰·洛克（1632-1704）描述了自然状态下的生活，这是一种想象的状态，人们共同生活在没有政府的环境中。

人在自然状态中是自由的。那么为什么他们愿意放弃这种自由，让自己受制于政府的权威？对于这个问题，显然可以这样回答：在自然状态中享有自由的权利是很不稳定的。人们总是不断地受到他人的侵犯。生活是危险的，充满恐惧。这就是为什么人们设法寻找那些愿意分享自己安全需求的人们，并加入他们。这样做是为了保护他们的生命、自由和财产。

为了确保一种稳妥的生活，自然状态有许多缺陷。第一，自然状态中缺少一种已经建立了的、所有人都同意并众所周知的法律体系。因为缺乏这样的法律，因此人们没有可以用来解决他们之间纠纷的是非标准。第二，自然状态中缺少拥有权威的裁判者来解决争端。第三，自然状态中缺少个人或者群体拥有权威来执行法律。

So then, this is why people join together under the protection and authority of government. This is why they agree on the administration of punishment according to the system of rules that the community has agreed on. This agreement is the source of legislative, judicial, and executive governmental authority.

Adapted from "On the Duty of Civil Disobedience" Henry David Thoreau (1849)

Henry David Thoreau, the American writer and essayist referred to in the last lesson, questioned whether government was needed at all.

I heartily accept this motto: "That government is best which governs least." I also believe the following: "that government is best which governs not at all." When people are ready for such a state of affairs, government will not be necessary at all.

There have been many good arguments made against having an army. These same arguments also can be made against having a government.

After all, the army is only an arm of the government. Governmental authority may easily be abused before the people can do anythingabout it.

A government does not have the energy or vitality of a single living person. The character of the American people has done all that has been accomplished in this country. Government never helped get anything done, except by getting out of people's way.

What do you think?

1. According to John Locke, what problems can arise when there is no government of authority?

2. What does Locke say is the source of governmental authority?

3. What was Thoreau's position about the need for governmental authority?

4. What changes in society would have to occur to make people ready to live without government?

因此，这就是为什么人们联合在一起处于政府的保护和权威之下。这就是为什么他们愿意按照社会所一致同意的规则体系来管理惩罚。这种一致同意就是立法、司法和执法的政府权威的起源。

摘自：《论公民的不服从》

作者：亨利·戴维·梭罗（1849年）

上一课中提到的美国作家及散文家亨利·戴维·梭罗提出了一个问题：人们是否真的需要政府？

我由衷地同意这个警句——"最好的政府是管得最少的政府"，我也相信其最终将是——"最好的政府是根本不进行治理的政府"。当人们对这样的事态做好准备后，政府将根本无需存在。

对设置常备军的反对意见很多、很强烈，同样地也有很多人反对设置政府。毕竟，常备军队不过是政府的一支胳臂，并且政府的权威也很容易在民众还没来得及运用它之前被可能被滥用。

政府的能量和活力还比不上一个活人。迄今为止，美国所有的成就全都由美国人民的性格造就。政府从未对此帮过任何忙，除了不挡人民的道以外。

你怎么看?

1. 根据洛克的描述，没有权威政府的时候会发生什么问题？
2. 对于政府权威的来源，洛克是怎么说的？
3. 对于政府权威的需求梭罗的观点是什么？
4. 社会中发生什么改变，人们才会愿意生活在没有政府的社会？

What are the uses of authority?

You have been reading about problems that may occur without adequate authority. How can authority be used to solve some of these problems? Authority has a number of important purposes:

- **Authority** can be used to protect important rights and freedoms. For example, the Constitution protects our freedoms of expression and belief.

- **Authority** can be used to ensure that resources and burdens will be distributed fairly. For example, our government sees that all children have an equal opportunity to receive a public education.

- **Authority** can be used to manage conflict peacefully and fairly. For example, our judicial system has the authority to provide a fair trial for a person accused of a crime.

 How is the authority of the Constitution used to protect freedom of religious beliefs? ☞

宪法权威是怎样用来保护宗教信仰自由的?

 How is the authority of the legal system used to manage conflict? ☞

法律体系的权威如何被用于解决争端?

权威的用途是什么?

上文中你们已经读到了,若没有适当的权威会出现什么问题。那么,如何运用权威来解决这些问题?权威有许多重要用途:

- **权威**可以用来保护重要的权利和自由。例如:宪法保护了我们表达和信仰的自由。
- **权威**可以用来确保资源和责任的公平分配。例如:我们的政府认为所有儿童都有平等接受公共教育的机会。
- **权威**可以被用于和平、公正地解决争端。例如:我们的司法体系有权威对被起诉的罪犯进行公平的审判。

Critical Thinking Exercise

EVALUATING THE USE OF AUTHORITY

For several years, the Reserve Mining Company of Silver Bay, Minnesota, had been dumping 67,000 tons of taconite waste into Lake Superior every day. In Duluth, Minnesota, sixty miles south of Silver Bay, research by the Environmental Protection Agency (EPA) showed high concentrations of cancer-causing fibers in the drinking water. The source of the drinking water was Lake Superior. The EPA traced the contamination directly to the Reserve Mining Company's waste emptied into the lake.

To find a solution to this problem, the Reserve Mining Company and the EPA held discussions. When negotiations failed, the case went to court. The EPA asked the court to order the immediate shutdown of the plant until those responsible could eliminate the pollution of Lake Superior. The company argued that it would cost too much money to obey the pollution control regulations demanded by the EPA. Furthermore, the company said that it would have to lay off 3,000 employees if they shut down the plant.

A federal court of appeals eventually decided that the taconite waste might contribute to cancer. The court ruled, however, that the pollution was not an immediate danger. The court gave the Reserve Mining Company three and a half years to stop polluting Lake Superior.

What do you think?

1. How was authority used to deal with the water supply contamination problem?

2. What problems might have arisen if there had beenno effective authority to deal with this situation?

3. In what other ways could authority have been used to deal with the problems in this situation?

重点思考练习

评估权威的运用

多年来，明尼苏达州银湾的储备矿业公司累计每天倾倒 67,000 吨铁燧岩废料到苏必利尔湖中。在银湾南面 60 公里处明尼苏达州的德卢斯，美国环境保护署（EPA）的研究表明，饮用水中有高浓度的致癌纤维，而该地饮用水的源头就是苏必利尔湖。环保署跟踪发现，污染物直接来源于储备矿业公司排入湖水中的废物。

为了找到解决这一问题的方法，储备矿业公司和环保署展开了讨论。双方谈判失败后，案件递交法院审理。环保署要求法院下令立即关闭工厂，直到工厂责任人可以消除苏必利尔湖的污染为止。储备矿业公司则认为，若按照环保署要求的污染控制规章，公司需要花费太多的钱。另外公司认为，关闭工厂将导致 3000 名工人失业。

地区联邦法院的最终判决是：铁燧岩废料可能导致癌症，但污染并非直接危险。法院判予储备矿业公司用 3 年半的时间停止对苏必利尔湖的污染。

你怎么看?

1. 在解决供水污染问题时，权威是如何被运用的？
2. 如果没有有效的权威去处理该问题，将会产生什么问题？
3. 在解决这一问题的过程中，还有什么别的途径来行使权威？

Using the Lesson

1. Consider all your actions today from the moment you woke up until you started reading this assignment. How many of your actions were governed by a rule or law? What was the purpose of each of these rules or laws? Do you think they were necessary? Record your answers to these questions in your journal.

2. Read the newspaper for several days. From your reading, make a list of problems that occurred due to lack of effective authority. After you have finished the list, suggest ways authority could have helped deal with these problems.

3. You have read what John Locke thought life would be like in a state of nature, that is, without government or laws; Do you agree or disagree with him? Write a story about what you think our life would be like in a state of nature.

知识运用

1. 从你今天醒来的那一刻开始到你读完这篇文章为止，思考这段时间里你的所有行动。当中有多少行为是在规则和法律控制之下的？这些规则或法律的目的是什么？你认为它们是必要的吗？在你的笔记中记下你对这些问题的答案。

2. 阅读这几天的报纸。从中找出一些因为缺乏有效权威而产生的问题。列出一份清单并思考行使权威可以有助于解决这些问题的方式，并给出你的建议。

3. 本课中你已经读过了洛克所描述的人们在自然状态（即没有政府或法律）中的生活，你是否同意他的观点？写一个故事，假设当你处于自然状态时，你的生活可能会是什么样的。

Unit Two

How Can We Evaluate Candidates for Positions of Authority?

Purpose of Unit

People who exercise authority oftevn have the right to control or influence our lives. Members of Congress, state legislatures, and city councils make many important laws. Police officers see that people follow laws. Teachers, principals, and parents make rules that influence the lives of young people.

We must choose people in positions of authority with great care because they can have a great influence on our lives. People who are well qualified to exercise authority can make our lives easier and more pleasant. Unqualified people in positions of authority can make our lives difficult and unpleasant.

Different positions of authority call for different qualifications Someone who is well qualified to be a police officer may not be qualified to be a judge. On the other hand, someone who makes a good judge might not make a good police officer. When selecting people to fill positions of authority, it is important to consider what qualifications they should have to be able to do their jobs well.

In this unit, you will learn some important steps to take when selecting people to fill positions of authority.

第二单元：我们如何评估权威职位的候选人？

> **单元目标**
>
> 那些行使权威的人通常有权利控制或影响我们的生活；国会议员、州议会和市政厅都制定了许多重要的法律，警察监督人们遵守法律，老师、校长和家长制定规则来影响年轻人的生活。

我们必须很小心地选择担任权威职位的人，因为他们会对我们的生活带来重要的影响。那些有良好资格行使权威的人可以让我们的生活变得更轻松、更愉快；而不称职的权威人物则会使我们的生活变得困苦不堪。

不同的权威职位要求候选人具备不同的资格。有些人更适合做警官，而不是做法官。另一方面，某些人能当个好法官，却可能无法成为一个好警察。在人们选择担任权威职位的人时，最需要考虑的是，为更好地完成这项工作，候选人应当具备哪些资格。

本单元中，你们将会学习许多重要步骤，来选择担任权威职位的人。

What qualifications should people have to fill different positions of authority?

担任不同权威职位的人应当具备哪些资格？

LESSON 4

How Should We Choose People for Positions of Authority?

Purpose of Lesson

This lesson introduces a set of intellectual tools that are useful in selecting people to fill positions of authority. These tools also are useful in evaluating the qualifications of persons who are in such positions.

When you have finished this lesson, you should be able to identify and explain the requirements of a position of authority. You also should be able to identify and explain the qualifications a person should possess to fill that position.

Terms to Know

position of authority	diligence
qualifications	abolitionist
woman suffrage	temperance

What qualities make a good leader?

Read the selection below then answer the What do you think?" questions. These questions will help you begin thinking about the characteristics a person should possess to fill a position of authority.

第四课：应当如何挑选担任权威职位的人？

本课目标

本课将介绍在挑选人才担任权威职位过程中很有用的一套知识工具。这些工具同样也有助于评估担任此类职位的人们的资格。当你们学完本课，你们应当能够明确并解释一个权威职位的工作要求，也应该能明确并阐述担任这一职位的人所应当具备的资格。

掌握词汇

权威职位	勤奋	资格
废奴主义者	妇女选举权	戒酒

什么素质造就了一位好的领袖？

阅读以下段落，并回答"你怎么看？"部分的问题。这些问题将会有助于你思考担任权威职位的人应当具备的特性。

Susan B. Anthony

Susan B. Anthony (1820-1906), abolitionist, temperance advocate, and most of all, champion of women's rights, held the strong conviction that women could never achieve their full rights until they first had won the right to vote. A skilled organizer, she played a key role in the passage of the Nineteenth Amendment giving women the right to vote. She was fearless in promoting the cause of women's rights and endured years of opposition and abuse as a result. The press slandered her, strangers jeered at her, and people often threw eggs and rotten fruit at her when she lectured.

Anthony grew up in a Quaker home and was a bright, independent child. She was well educated and spent a number of years teaching. Her interests, however, lay in other areas and she soon became deeply involved in the moral crusades that would absorb her time and energy for years. At a time when people expected women to stay home, she used her intelligence, determination, and organizational skills to further the causes in which she believed. Discouraged by the limited role allowed to women in the temperance movement, she helped found the Woman's State Temperance Society of New York. She also served as an agent for the American Anti-Slavery Society. Her prime concern, however, was to further the rights of women. Anthony was one of the foremost leaders in the movement for woman suffrage, and in 1892 she was elected president of the National American Woman Suffrage Association.

 What qualities should a person possess to be a successful leader or advocate for community change? ☞

苏珊·安东尼

苏珊·安东尼（1820 — 1906）是一位废除死刑和禁酒令的倡导者、妇女权利的捍卫者。她坚信妇女必须首先赢得投票权，否则就无法充分行使自己的权利。作为一名经验老道的活动组织者，苏珊的关键影响使宪法第十九修正案得以通过并给予了美国妇女投票权。在推进妇女权利的过程中，虽然长期遭受敌视和辱骂，她也无所畏惧——新闻界诬蔑她，陌生人嘲笑她，人们常在她发表演讲时向她投掷鸡蛋和烂水果。

安东尼在一个贵格教徒的家庭里长大，是一个聪明、独立的孩子。她受过良好教育，当过几年教师。然而她很快对道德运动领域产生了兴趣，并很快投身其中，付出了多年的时间和精力。在那个人们普遍认为妇女应该待在家里做贤妻良母的年代，苏珊用她的智慧、决心和组织能力，将她所坚信的事业逐步推进。有感于妇女在禁酒运动中发挥的作用有限，她协助创建了纽约州妇女禁酒协会。她同时还是美国反奴隶制协会的成员。但她最关心的还是要进一步推进妇女的权利。安东尼是争取妇女选举权运动中最重要的领袖之一，1892 年她当选为全美争取妇女投票权协会的主席。

一个成功的领导者或社区变革的倡导者，应当具备什么资格？

In November 1872, police arrested Anthony as she attempted to vote in the presidential election. A few months later, she compounded her crime by trying to vote in a city election. Although she was convicted, she refused to pay the fine. Neither public ridicule nor the fear of jail could deter her commitment to the cause in which she so fervently believed.

Anthony assisted in organizing international woman suffrage associations, helped compile and publish a history of the suffrage movement, and spoke tirelessly throughout the country on the subject of women's rights for more than half a century. She died in 1906, only a few years before her dream of woman suffrage became a reality.

What do you think?

1. What were the responsibilities of a position of authority in the woman suffrage movement?

2. What characteristics did Anthony have that helped make her a successful leader?

How should we choose someone for a position of authority?

In the preceding activity, you listed some responsibilities of a position of authority and the characteristics necessary to do the job well. You often will have the opportunity to select people for positions of authority. To make wise choices, you will need some intellectual tools. Just as there are tools with which to repair a car or bake a cake, there are tools of the mind with which to examine issues.

Intellectual tools include a variety of ideas, observations about society and our roles within it, and sets of questions that are useful in analyzing situations and reaching decisions. The following are some intellectual tools you can use when deciding if someone is qualified for a particular position.

1. WHAT ARE THE DUTIES, POWERS, PRIVILEGES, AND LMITATIONS OF THE POSITION?

Before you can decide how qualified a person is for a position, you must first consider what the job involves.

1872 年 11 月，由于苏珊试图在总统选举中投票，警方逮捕了她。几个月后，她又因试图在市议会选举中投票而加重了自己的罪行。虽然她被法院判定有罪，但却拒绝支付罚金。无论是公众的嘲笑还是牢狱之灾，都无法阻止她献身于自己所狂热追求和信仰的事业当中。

安东尼协助组织了国际妇女参政协会，参与编辑并出版了有关妇女争取投票权运动的历史书籍，并在近半个世纪的时间里坚持在全美各地发表关于妇女权利问题的演讲。1906 年苏珊·安东尼逝世，几年后，她为妇女争取选举权的梦想成为了现实。

你怎么看？

1. 在妇女争取投票权运动中的权威职位有哪些责任？
2. 安东尼具备什么特性使她成为一位成功的领导者？

应当如何选择担任权威职位的人？

之前你们已经列举了某些权威职位应当承担的责任，以及做好这项工作应当具备的特性。以后你们将有很多机会选择担任权威职位的人。为了做出明智的选择，你们需要一些知识工具。就像有专门用来修理汽车或烘焙蛋糕的工具一样，研究问题也需要智慧的工具。

知识工具包括一系列关于社会的想法和意见，以及对于我们在社会中的角色的想法和意见；知识工具也包括一系列有助于分析具体情况和作出决定的问题。当你们需要思考一个人是否适合某个特定职位时，可以使用以下知识工具：

1. 这个职位的职责、权力、特权和限制是什么？

在判断一个人是否适合某个职位之前，你们必须首先考虑这份工作涉及到哪些内容。

2. WHAT CHARACTERISTICS SHOULD A PERSON HAVE TO BE SELECTED FOR THE POSITION?

The characteristics of the person for a particular job should enable that individual to fulfill the duties and powers of that position and to do the job well. Depending on the position, some characteristics that might be important include the following:

- specialized knowledge or skills

- physical capacity

- impartiality

- integrity

- intelligence

- diligence

- reliability

- courage

- ability to work with other people

- sensitivity to human needs and rights

- views on job-related issues

3. WHAT ARE THE STRENGTHS AND WEAKNESSES OF THE PERSONS BEING CONSIDERED FOR THE POSITION?

Each candidate's characteristics should be compared with the qualities needed for the job as well as with the characteristics of the other candidates.

4. WHICH PERSON WOULD BEST FILL THE POSITION? WHY?

You should be able to explain the basis for your selection using the information gained from answering the first three questions in the procedure.

2. 担任这个职位的人应当具备什么特性？

担任某个特定职位的人所具备的特性，应当能帮助个人顺利完成工作，并履行其职责、行使权力。

某些重要的特性是依据具体职位而定的，其中包括：
- 专业知识或技能
- 身体素质
- 公正
- 诚实
- 有智慧
- 勤奋
- 可靠、可信赖
- 勇敢
- 能与他人共事
- 尊重他人的需要和权利
- 对与工作有关的问题有自己的观点

3. 担任这一职位的候选人有什么优点和缺点？

应该将每个候选人的特性与该职位所需要具备的资格进行对比，同时也与其他候选人的特性进行比较。

4. 谁最适合这个职位？为什么？

通过回答前三个问题所获得的信息，你应当能够说明你所做出的选择及其理由。

Critical Thinking Exercise

EVALUATING CHARACTERISTICS OF A WELL-QUALIFIED PRESIDENT

The following activity provides you with an opportunity to apply the intellectual tools you have just learned. Working in small groups, read the excerpt from Article II of the Constitution describing the position of president of the United States. Then work with your group to complete the chart on p. 70. Be prepared to share your answers with the class.

Article II

Section 1. Before he enter on the Execution of his Office, he shall take the following Oath or Affirmation: "I do solemnly swear (or affirm) that I will faithfully execute the Office of President of the United States, and will to the best of my Ability, preserve, protect and defend the Constitution of the United States."

Section 2. The President shall be Commander in Chief of the Army and Navy of the United States, and of the Militia of the several States ...and he shall have Power to grant Reprieves and Pardons for Offenses against the United States, except in Cases of Impeachment.

How do the duties, powers, privileges, and limitations of a position of authority help you decide what characteristics a person needs to have to fill it? ☞

重点思考练习

评估一个合格的总统的特性

下面你们将有机会用到刚刚所学的知识工具。分小组阅读宪法第二条中关于总统的职位描述。各小组一起完成第 71 页的表格，准备与全班分享你们的答案。

第二条

第一款　总统在开始执行职务前，应作如下宣誓或宣言："我庄严宣誓（或宣言）我一定忠实执行合众国总统职务，竭尽全力维护、保护和捍卫合众国宪法。"

第二款　总统是合众国陆军、海军和征调为合众国服役的各州民兵的总司令。……他有权对危害合众国的犯罪行为发布缓刑令和赦免令，但弹劾案除外。

某个权威职位的责任、权力、特权和限制如何帮助你确定担任这一职位的人需要具备的特性？

He shall have Power, by and with the Advice and Consent of the Senate, to make Treaties, provided two thirds of the Senators present concur; and he shall nominate, and by and with the Advice and Consent of the Senate, shall appoint Ambassadors, other public Ministers and Consuls, Judges of the Supreme Court, and all other Officers of the United States, whose Appointments are not herein otherwise provided for, and which shall be established by Law: but the Congress may by Law vest the Appointment of such inferior Officers, as they think proper, in the President alone, in the Courts of Law, or in the Heads of Departments.

The President shall have Power to fill up all Vacancies that may happen during the Recess of the Senate, by granting Commissions which shall expire at the End of their next Session.

Section 3.

What do you think?

1. What characteristics should a person have to be selected for the position of president?

2. Think about the characteristics you identified for Susan B. Anthony that qualified her to lead the woman suffrage movement. What similarities do you see between those characteristics and the ones you have identified for the presidency? What characteristics are different

---

Using the lesson

1. Choose a television program that shows someone in a position of authority. Write the duties, powers, privileges, and limitations of the position. Then describe the characteristics of the person in that job that qualify him or her for the position. Explain whether or not you would select this person for the position.

2. Think of a position of authority you might like to serve in some day. In your journal, write a short description of the position, the characteristics someone should possess to do it well, and explain why you might qualify for the job.

总统经咨询参议院和取得其同意有权缔结条约，但须经出席参议员三分之二的批准。他提名，并经咨询参议院和取得其同意，任命大使、公使和领事、最高法院法官和任命手续未由本宪法另行规定而应由法律规定的合众国所有其他官员。但国会认为适当时，可以法律将这类低级官员的任命权授予总统一人、法院或各部部长。

总统有权委任人员填补在参议院休会期间可能出现的官员缺额，此项委任在参议院下期会议结束时满期。

第三款

总统应不时向国会报告联邦情况，并向国会提出他认为必要和妥善的措施供国会审议。在非常情况下，他得召集两院或任何一院开会。如遇两院对休会时间有意见分歧时，他可使两院休会到他认为适当的时间。他应接见大使和公使。他应负责使法律切实执行，并委任合众国的所有官员。

你怎么看？

1. 一个人应当具备什么特性才能当选总统？
2. 回想之前所列举的有关苏珊·安东尼适合领导妇女争取投票权运动的特性。对比第一个问题中你们认为适合担任总统职位的特性，两者之间有哪些相同点？有哪些不同？

知识运用

1. 选择一档内容有关担任权威职位的个人的电视节目，写下这一职位的职责、权力、特权和限制。然后描述他或她适合担任这项工作的特性。解释你是否会选择这个人担任这一权威职位。
2. 设想你将来可能担任的权威职位。在你的笔记本上对这一职位进行简单的描述，并说明要很好地完成这项工作所应当具备的特性，并解释为什么你会适合这份工作。

Duties, Powers, Privileges, and Limitations of the Position of President	Characteristics a President Should Have
Questions	Answers
Duties and Power. The president has the duty and power to • give Congress periodic information on the state of the Union • make sure that the laws of the land are faithfully executed • command the armed forces • appoint judqes to the Supreme Court • appoint the heads of the executive departments • preserve, protect, and defend the Constitution of the United States	To perform these duties and exercise these powers, the president should be
Privileges. The president has the following privileges: • receives a substantial salary and expense allowance • uses special air and ground transportation • lives in the White House and has the use of Camp David • receives protection by the Secret Service • receives the assistance of the Cabinet and other members of the executive department • receives free medical care	To be trusted with these privileges, the president should be
Limitations. The president may not do the following: • serve more than two terms of office • engage in treason, bribery, or other high crimes and misdemeanors • violate the Constitution of the United States	To comply with these limitations, the president should bet

总统职位的责任、权力、特权和限制	一个总统应当具备的特性
问题	答案
责任和权力——总统有责任和权力： ・向国会定期提交国情咨文 ・确保土地法得以切实执行 ・指挥军队 ・任命最高法院法官 ・委任行政各部门官员 ・维护、保护和捍卫美国宪法	为履行这些责任和行使这些权力，总统应当：
特权——总统拥有以下特权： ・有一笔可观的工资收入和津贴 ・使用特殊的空中和地面交通工具 ・住在白宫和有权使用戴维营 ・受到特工处保护 ・得到内阁和行政部门其他成员的协助 ・享受免费医疗服务	被赋予这些特权，总统应当：
限制——总统不能做以下事： ・任期超过两届 ・从事叛国、贿赂或其他重罪和轻罪 ・违反美国宪法	为了遵守这些限制，总统应当：

LESSON 5
Who Would You Select for This Position of Authority?

> ### Purpose of Lesson
>
> This lesson gives you an opportunity to use the intellectual tools you have just studied to decide which candidate is most qualified for a position of authority. When you have completed the lesson, you should be able to explain what considerations you used to justify the choices you made.

Terms to Know

levying

pollution

welfare program

Critical Thinking Exercise

TAKING A POSITION ON A CANDIDATE FOR PUBLIC OFFICE

In this exercise you will select a person to serve in your state legislature. Your class will conduct Editorial Board Endorsement Interviews in which reporters and editors of the city's daily newspaper question four candidates for the position. To prepare for this exercise, read the description of Central City and the "Memorandum to the People of Central City." Then follow the "Instructions for Conducting the Editorial Board Endorsement Interviews" that follow the memorandum.

第五课：应当选择谁来担任权威职位？

本课目标

　　本课中你们将有机会运用刚学到的知识工具，来决定哪个候选人最适合担任某个权威职位。学完本课后，你们应当能够说明自己所考虑的因素，用来证明自己的选择。

掌握词汇

征税

污染

福利计划

重点思考练习

评选公职机关候选人

　　在本次练习中，你将选出一位将在你所在州的议会工作的人。你们班将模拟本地城市日报的记者和编辑，对这一职位的四位候选人进行"编辑委员会认可面试"。为准备此次练习，阅读有关"中心市"的描述和"中心市市民备忘录"。然后按照材料后面的"编辑委员会认可面试"的说明，对候选人进行面试。

Central City

Central City is a large city located in the midwest region of the United States. The city is largely industrialized with a variety of manufacturing plants located throughout the town. These manufacturing plants provide jobs for many people who live in Central City.

The central part of the city has many problems. The crime rate is high; housing and school facilities are substandard, and there is a large amount of unemployment, drug use, violence, and pollution.

Central City has thirty-three elementary schools, twenty junior high schools, and seventeen high schools. Students attend these schools from the entire county. The county government just built a new hospital with some help from the state.

The city contains two major parks and there is a state park just a few miles away. In the winter, the parks are good places for sledding and ice skating; in summer, people use them for picnics, swimming, and baseball.

 What qualifications should a person have to govern a large municipality? ☞

中心市

中心市是美国中西部地区的一个大城市，这个工业化城市中遍布着各种各样的制造工厂，这些工厂为中心市许多居民提供了就业机会。

市区中部有很多社会问题：较高的犯罪率，不合标准的住房和学校设施，还有大量的失业人员、吸毒、暴力犯罪和工业污染。

中心市有 33 所小学、20 所初中和 17 所高中。学生们从各地来到这里。政府刚刚在州政府的帮助下新建了一所医院。

市区有两个大公园，离市区几英里远有一个国家公园。冬季，公园是乘雪橇和滑冰的好地方；夏天，人们在公园里野餐、游泳、打棒球。

管理一座大城市的人应当具备什么资格？

A system of high ways that was built with state and federal taxes connects Central City to other communities. Central City has a municipal government. Every four years the people elect a mayor and a city council to provide local government for the city. The voters in the city also have the right to elect a representative to the state legislature every two years. The state legislature has the authority to perform certain duties, including the following:

- **Levying taxes.** The legislature has the authority to tax personal incomes and place a sales tax on some items that people buy.

- **Deciding how to spend tax money.** The legislature has the authority to decide how to spend the state's tax money. In the past, they used tax money for such things as schools, state highways, state parks, wildlife preserves, dams, and water systems. They also used it to aid farmers and people who were poor or disabled.

- **Passing new legislation.** The legislature has the authority to make or change the laws of the state. For example, members of the state legislature pass laws that do the following:

- define what actions will be considered crimes

- govern the owning, licensing, and driving of automobiles

- regulate the qualifications necessary for certain professions

- affect school curricula

- **Deciding on minimum wage levels and employee benefits.** The legislature has the authority to decide the minimum hourly wage rate and any allowable exceptions. It also can decide the kinds of benefits employers must provide for their workers. These benefits include paid sick leave, maternity leave, and payment for injuries that happen on the job.

用本州和联邦税收修建的高速公路系统将中心市与其他城区连接起来。中心市有自己的市政府，每四年全市人民选出新一任市长和市议会，组建成中心市政府。每两年中心市的选民也有权选出代表进入州议会。州议会有权行使某些职责，包括：

征税。州议会有权征收个人所得税，同时对人们购买某些商品征税。

决定如何使用税款。州议会有权决定如何使用州的税款。州议会通常将这些税款用于学校、州立高速公路、国家公园、野生动物保护区、水坝和供水系统。州议会也会使用税款来帮助农民、穷人或残疾人。

批准新的立法。州议会有权制定或改变州的法律。例如，州议会议员通过批准法律来：
· 确定何种行为将被视为犯罪
· 管理车辆的持有、执照和驾驶
· 规范某些职业的必要资格
· 调整学校课程

决定最低工资水平和员工福利。州议会有权决定最低小时工资率和任何可允许的例外规定。同时，州议会也可以决定雇主必须为其员工提供的各种福利，其中包括带薪病假、产假和支付工伤损失。

Memorandum to the People of Central City

FROM: THE LEAGUE OF VOTERS   SUBJECT: NEXT WEEK'S ELECTION

Since we believe that next week's election is important, we have prepared the following information for your consideration. We hope that you will find it helpful when choosing among the candidates.

Our legislator has the duty and power to do the following:

- work for the good of all people of Central City
- attend meetings of the state legislature
- serve on committees
- conduct and participate in hearings
- propose new laws
- vote on proposed new laws
- give fair consideration to the needs and interests of other communities in the state

To fulfill these duties and powers, our legislator should do the following:

- know the interests of all the people and be willing to work for the good of everyone
- be reliable, attend as many meetings as possible, and be at meetings on time
- work well with others and be able to compromise, bargain, .and persuade
- be well prepared, open-minded, a good listener, and a good questioner
- be skilled in creating and writing new laws
- consider the welfare of all the people of Central City and the rest of the state
- be fair when the interests of Central City conflict with the interests of other communities

As privileges of office, our legislator is entitled to the following:

- an income of $45,000 per year
- exemption from libel or slander lawsuits for anything said while on the floor of the legislature:

To receive these privileges, our legislator should do the following:

- be diligent and devote the time necessary to earn the salary for the position
- speak with good taste and discretion

As limitations of office, our legislator cannot do the following:

- hold or be paid for other jobs while serving as a legislator
- vote on bills in which there is any conflict of interest
- work to pass laws that are prohibited by the Constitution of the United States or the constitution of our state

To fulfill these limitations, our legislator should do the following:

- be honest and trustworthy and refuse money for outside work
- avoid voting on bills in which he or she has any personal interest
- know and support the basic principles of both the U.S. and our state constitutions

中心市市民备忘录

来自：选民联盟　　主题：下周的竞选

我们认为下周的选举很重要，因此准备了以下资料供大家参考。我们希望这份材料将会有助于你在各位候选人中做出选择。

我们的议员有责任和权力去做：

- 为中心市的所有人民的利益工作
- 出席州议会的各项会议
- 担任委员会成员
- 举行并参加听证会
- 提出新的法律提案
- 针对新的法律提案进行投票
- 对州内其他地区的需要和利益给予公平考虑

为了履行这些职责和权力，我们的议员应该做到以下内容：

- 了解所有人民的利益，并愿意为每个人的利益服务
- 是可信赖的人，尽可能准时出席更多的会议
- 与他人合作，并能向他人妥协、与他人谈判和说服其他人
- 做好了充分的准备、思想开放、善于倾听和提问
- 能熟练制定和撰写新的法律提案
- 考虑到中心城市和州内其他地区所有居民的福祉
- 当中心市的利益和其他地区的利益发生冲突时能保持公平

由于政府机关的特权，我们的议员有资格享有：

- 年收入45,000美元
- 免于任何诽谤和污蔑的诉讼，呈递法庭的案件除外

要获得这些特权，我们的议员应该做到以下几点：

- 勤奋，贡献必要的时间赚取相应职位的工资
- 语言优雅，并具有决断力

出于对政府机关的限制，议员不能做以下事：

- 在担任议员期间担任其他工作，或因其他工作收取报酬
- 对存在利益冲突的法案进行表决
- 批准美国宪法或本州宪法所禁止的法案

为了服从这些限制，我们的议员应该做到以下几点：

- 诚实守信，拒绝来自其他工作的金钱
- 避免参与任何有关他或她个人利益的法案的投票
- 了解和支持美国和本州宪法的基本准则

Instructions for Conducting the Editorial Board Endorsement Interviews

Your teacher will divide your class into five groups. One group will represent the members of the Central City Daily Journal editorial board. Each of the other groups will represent one of the four candidates for the office of state legislator. Each group should follow the directions below to prepare for the Editorial Board Endorsement Interviews.

Students should follow a "meet the press" format in which the editorial board interviews the four candidates. After each candidate has made an opening statement, members of the editorial board may ask questions. Other members of each candidate group may assist their candidate in responding to questions.

Group 1: Editorial Board Group

You represent the editorial board of the Central City Daily Journal, the largest newspaper in Central City, Your board will endorse one of the candidates for state representative and your endorsement will give a substantial boost to the campaign of the candidate you select.

Your group should read and discuss the candidate profiles that follow. List the strengths and weaknesses of each candidate. To help you with this task, refer to the description of Central City. You also should look at the memorandum that outlines the responsibilities of a state legislator and the characteristics that a person should have to fill that position.

 How can televised debates and news media interviews help us evaluate candidates for positions of authority? ☞

进行"编辑委员会认可面试"的说明：

老师将把你们班分成五组。其中一组将代表《中心市日报》编辑委员会，其他各组将分别代表竞选州议员的四位候选人。每个小组都应按照以下说明来准备"编辑委员会认可面试"。

在编辑委员会面试 4 位候选人时，同学们应当采用类似"新闻发布会"的流程，在每位候选人做完各自的开场发言后，编辑部成员开始提问。候选人小组的其他成员可以在回答问题时协助自己小组的候选人。

第一组：编辑委员会组

你们代表了中心市最大的报社——《中心市日报》。你们的编辑委员会将选出一名州议员的候选人，而你们小组的认可将极大地支持该候选人的竞选。

你们组应仔细阅读并讨论下文中的候选人简介，并列出每一位候选人的优势和劣势。为更好地完成这个任务，请参阅上文的中心市简介。同时你们也应仔细阅读市民备忘录，当中概述了一个州议员的职责和担任此职位的人所应当具备的特性。

电视辩论和新闻媒体的采访报道将如何能有助于我们评估权威职位的候选人？

Prepare a list of questions to ask each candidate. You will have about five minutes to question each candidate after he or she has presented an opening statement of three to four minutes. Your questions should probe the candidates about their ability to fulfill the responsibilities of the position.

Select a chairperson to conduct the interviews. The chairperson will explain the procedure to the candidates. The chairperson also will moderate the discussion period after each candidate's opening statement. Note that other members of each candidate group can assist their candidate in responding to questions.

Group 2: Candidate Groups

Your group should read and discuss the profile of your candidate. List your candidate's strengths and weaknesses. To help you with this task, refer to the description of Central City and the "Memorandum to the People of Central City."Your group should then choose one member to play the candidate. Help that person get ready for the editorial board interview; prepare a short opening statement in which your candidate will try to convince the editorial board that he or she has the characteristics required to perform the job well. The group also should help the candidate rehearse answers to possible questions from the editorial board. Remember to stress why he or she is the best candidate for the position. Other group members will be allowed to help the candidate in the question-and-answer period.

列出一系列问题，以便询问每一位候选人。在每位候选人各自 3 至 4 分钟的开场发言后，你们将有 5 分钟的时间问问题，这些问题应当能准确地检测候选人在履行工作职能方面的能力。

选出一位同学担任编辑委员会主席，并主持面试。主席将向各位候选人解释面试流程，并在每位候选人的开场致辞后主持讨论。请注意，每个候选人小组的其他成员可以帮助候选人回答问题。

第二组：候选人小组

你们应该仔细读并讨论你们组候选人的简介，列出他或她的优势和劣势。　为更好地完成这个任务，请参阅上文的中心市简介和中心市市民备忘录。

接下来，你们组应该选出一名组员来扮演候选人，其他组员应帮助这位同学准备编辑委员会的面试。为你们的候选人准备一个简短的开场致辞。在开场发言中。候选人要尽力向编辑委员会证明自己具备了顺利完成这项工作的资格。你们组还应该帮助候选人模拟回答编辑委员会可能提出的问题。请记住，要强调为什么你们组的候选人是这个职位的最佳人选。在问答阶段，其他小组成员可以帮助候选人回答。

Candidate Profiles

Raul Garcia

Background: Raul was born and raised in Central City. He is married and has three grown children. Raul's wife, Sue, works in the General Clothing Store on Elm Street.

Employment: Raul has worked in a manufacturing plant since he was seventeen and has advanced to the position of foreman. Raul was one of the first workers at the plant to join. Some say he is largely responsible for union workers getting higher pay and more benefits.

Position on the issues: Raul believes the minimum wage for workers is too low and that they need more benefits such as a better medical plan. He also thinks that the state should pass a law requiring that employers pay for more of these benefits.

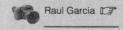 Raul Garcia ☞

候选人简介

劳尔 · 加西亚

背景：劳尔出生、成长在中心市，已婚，有三个已成年的孩子。劳尔的妻子苏 · 加西亚在埃尔姆街一家服装店工作。

职业：劳尔从 17 岁起就在一家制造厂工作，并被提升为工头。劳尔是工厂里的第一批参政的工人之一。有些人说，他这样做主要是为了给工会的工人们争取更高的薪水和更多的福利。

劳尔 · 加西亚

政见：劳尔认为，工人们的最低工资太低，他们需要更多的福利，例如一个更好的医疗计划。他还认为，州议会应当通过一项法律，要求雇主为工人们的福利支付更多钱。

Jennifer Brown

Background: Jennifer was born in Central City, but when she was young, her family moved to a nearby town. She received her law degree at the state university and returned to Central City to practice law.

Employment: Jennifer is a partner in one of the largest law firms in Central City. She handles all kinds of cases. When workers were first organizing a union, Jennifer worked to protect their rights. Later, when the union made demands for higher wages and greater benefits, the industry hired her to argue their side of the issue. Jennifer is a member of the State Bar Association and the Chamber of Commerce.

Position on the issues: Jennifer is interested in problems on both the local and state levels. She believes that her experience in practicing law will help her be an effective legislator. She also thinks that laws controlling industrial pollution are neither fair to industry nor effective in protecting the environment. She wants to improve these laws.

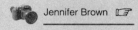 Jennifer Brown ☞

珍妮弗·布朗

珍妮弗·布朗

　　背景：珍妮弗出生于中心市，但在她小时候全家搬到了中心市附近的一个小镇上居住。她在州立大学获得法学学位后回到中心市进入法律界工作。

　　职业：珍妮弗是在中心市最大的一家律师事务所的合伙人。她处理过各种案子。中心市工人首次组织工会时，珍妮弗致力于保护他们的权利。后来工会提出了高工资和更多福利的要求，工业界聘请她为雇主一方游说。珍妮弗是州立律师公会和商会的成员。

　　政见：珍妮弗对本地和州内事务都很关注。她相信自己在法律事务中的经验将帮助她成为一个有能力的议员。她也认为，现有的控制工业污染的法律既对工业的发展不公平，也无法有效地保护环境。她希望能改善这些法律。

Patricia Chang

Background: Pat was born and raised in Central City. She is married, has one child, and has been active in the PTA and in women's groups.

Employment: Pat has taught American history and American government at Central City High School for eleven years. She has been head of the social studies department for the past four years. Students like her and other teachers respect her. Pat is a member of the Social Studies Teachers Association.

Position on the issues: Pat believes that public education needs more state support. She thinks that increasing teachers' salaries and reducing the number of students in each class would be beneficial. She is concerned about environmental pollution, especially from the local cement plant. Pat thinks there should be strict state laws to control pollution. She also believes that the legislature should spend more money on welfare programs.

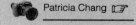 Patricia Chang ☞

帕特里夏·张

背 景：帕特出生、成长在中心市。她已婚，有一个孩子，并在教师——家长协会和各种妇女团体中表现活跃。

职 业：帕特在中心市高中教授美国历史和美国政府课程长达 11 年。过去四年中她曾担任社会科学系主任一职。学生们喜欢她，其他老师尊重她。帕特也是社会科学教师协会的成员。

帕特里夏·张

政 见：帕特认为，公共教育需要更多州政府的支持，提高教师的工资和减少每个班级的学生人数都将有助于改善公共教育。她关注环境污染问题，特别是当地水泥厂这一污染源。帕特主张应当有严格的法律来控制污染。她也认为州议会应该花更多的钱在福利计划上。

William Bill Meyers

Background: Bill is married and has three children who are still in school. He and his wife were born on farms in a nearby county. Bill and his family love the parks and lakes around Central City.

Employment: When he graduated from high school, Bill began working in the Cement Block and Pipe Company. He has been manager of that company for ten years. People consider Bill to be a good and efficient manager. Bill is past-president of the Chamber of Commerce and the Central City Fish and Game Club.

Position on the issues: Bill thinks that employers and employees should agree on workers' salaries and benefits without regulation from the state. He does not favor increased spending for welfare; he believes local charities should take care of such needs. He believes that the state should spend more money on wildlife preserves and state parks.

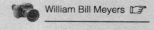 William Bill Meyers ☞

威廉·比尔·迈尔斯

威廉·比尔·迈尔斯

背景：比尔已婚，家里有三个孩子都还在学校念书。他和他的妻子都出生在中心市附近县城的农场。比尔和他的家人很喜欢中心市周围的公园和湖泊。

职业：比尔高中毕业后就开始在水泥和管道公司工作。他已经在该公司担任了 10 年经理职务。人们认为比尔是一个很善良、很有能力的经理。比尔是商会和中心市渔猎俱乐部的前任主席。

政见：比尔认为，雇主和雇员应该在一致同意的基础上确定工人的工资和福利而非依靠国家调控。他并不赞成增加福利开支，他认为本地慈善机构应当负责这种需要。他主张国家应该花更多的钱建立野生动物保护区和国家公园。

Which candidate will you endorse?

After the editorial board has completed the interviews, it should select a candidate to endorse for the position of state legislator. When making its selection, the editorial board should consider the following questions:

• What are the strengths and weaknesses of each candidate running for the office?

• Which candidate do you think is best qualified to be a state legislator?

The chairperson of the editorial board should announce the boards' decision to the class, and explain the reasons for the board's endorsement of the candidate it chose. The class as a whole may then conduct a mock election for the position of state representative.

Using the Lesson

1. Pick a candidate for state legislature other than the one the editorial board selected. Write a letter to the editor of the Central City Daily Journal defending your choice of candidate for the legislature.

2. Compare the candidates from the last presidential election using the criteria you have learned in this unit. Write a script for a thirty-second long television commercial for the candidate of your choice.

你们会选择哪一位候选人?

编辑委员会在面试后应选出一位候选人去竞选州议员的席位。在选择的过程中，编辑委员会应当考虑以下问题：

- 竞选公职的各位候选人都有哪些优势和劣势？
- 你认为哪位候选人最有资格成为州议员？

编辑委员会主席应向全班宣布委员会的最终决定，并解释委员会认可并选择这位候选人的原因。然后可以全班一起进行一场竞选州议员的模拟选举。

知识运用

1. 在编辑委员会决定的人选之外选择一位候选人，写一封信给中心市日报社的编辑，为你的议员候选人进行辩护。

2. 运用在本单元学到的标准，对比去年参加总统竞选的候选人，为你选定的候选人写一篇 30 秒电视广告的脚本。

Unit Three

How Can We Evaluate Rules and Laws?

> ### Purpose of Unit
>
> You have learned that sometimes it is helpful to give certain people the right to exercise authority. Most positions of authority involve rules. Some people in positions of authority make rules. Others enforce them. Still others settle arguments about the meaning of rules and decide what to do with people who have disobeyed them.

In our democratic system, people we elect to public office have a right to make rules or laws. They make many laws to protect people's rights. They make other laws that are supposed to ensure that all citizens receive their fair share of community resources.

Some people think that just because a rule exists, it must be a good rule. This is not always so. Rules can have many things wrong with them. It is not always easy to make a good rule. In this unit you will learn how to evaluate whether a rule is good or not You also will learn how to improve rules and how to develop good rules.

第三单元：如何评估规则和法律？

> ## 单元目标
>
> 你们已经学到有时赋予某些人权利去行使权力是有帮助的。大部分权威职位都涉及到规则。某些拥有权威职位的人制定规则，另外一些负责执行，还有一些人负责解决有关规则定义的争论，并决定如何处理不遵守规则的人。

在美国的民主体系中，我们选出的担任公共职务的人有权利制定规则或法律。他们制定了许多法律用来保护人民的权利，也制定其他法律用以确保所有公民能公平地分享社会资源。

有些人认为，既然社会中存在某种规则，那么这种规则一定是好的。事情往往并非如此。规则也通常伴随着许多错误。制定一项好的规则并不是件容易的事。在本单元中，你们将学习如何评估规则的好坏，也将学习如何健全规章制度，以及如何建立良好的规则。

How can you evaluate whether a rule or law is good?

我们如何评估某项规则或法律是好的？

LESSON 6

What Should You Consider When Evaluating Rules?

Purpose of Lesson

This lesson introduces you to some intellectual tools useful in making and evaluating rules and laws. When you have completed the lesson, you should be able to use these tools to evaluate rules and to suggest ways to improve them.

Terms to Know

characteristics
criteria
hypothetical

What makes a rule well designed?

Think about how important rules and laws are in your life. Since they are so important, we need to make sure that the rules we follow are well designed.

• What might happen if a rule is not well designed?

• What criteria would you use to evaluate a rule?

Critical Thinking Exercise

IDENTIFYING WHATISWRONG WITH THESE RULES

Each of the following hypothetical rules has a problem or weakness. Thinking about how to correct these weaknesses will help you identify some criteria or standards for evaluating rules. As you read each example, write what you think is wrong with the rule. After completing all six examples, make a list of the characteristics or qualities you think a rule should have by completing the sentence, "A good rule should be ...". Be prepared to share your answers with the class.

第六课：评估规则时应当考虑哪些因素？

本课目标

　　本课将向你们介绍一些有助于制定和评估规则与法律的知识工具。学完本课后，你们应该能运用这些工具来评估规则，并对如何改善规则提出自己的建议。

掌握词汇

　　特性

　　标准

　　假设

什么使一项规则得到精心设计？

　　试想一下，在你的生活中规则和法律有多么重要。而正是由于它们的重要性，我们需要确保自己所遵循的规则是经过精心设计的。

　　如果规则没有得到很好的设计会发生什么事？

　　你会用什么标准来评估某项规则？

重点思考练习

找出这些规则有什么问题

　　以下每一种假设的规则都存在一个问题或缺陷。思考如何纠正这些错误，将有助于了解评估规则的一些标准。在阅读每个案例时，写下你认为错误的地方。读完 6 个案例后，按照以下句式列出你认为一个规则所应当具备的特性或品质："一个好的规则应当是……"。准备与全班分享你的答案。

1. To qualify to vote, a citizen must own at least ten acres or $10,000 worth of property.

2. No person shall, may, or will, unnecessarily, or without cause, fustigate another person's cranial orb or any other segment of his corporeal being, whatsoever.

3. To promote health and fitness, a new federal law allows only those citizens weighing 145 pounds or less to vote presidential elections.

4. Anyone who uses too much water will have to pay a fine.

5. Police and other government officials may search a person's home whenever they feel like it.

6. All students must eat twenty-eight hamburgers for lunch every day.

1. 为了具备投票资格，一个公民必须拥有至少 10 英亩土地，或 10000 美元财产。

2. 任何人不应该、不可以或不会在无关紧要和毫无原因的情况下，用棍棒击打另一个人的头颅或身体的其他任何部分。

3. 为了促进健康和健美，一项新的联邦法律只允许体重小于（含）145 磅的公民参与总统竞选投票。

4. 任何过多用水的人将不得不为此支付罚款。

5. 警察及其他政府官员可以搜索一个人的家，无论对方是否愿意。

6. 所有学生每天中午必须吃 28 个汉堡包。

How can you evaluate a rule?

As a citizen in a democracy, you will have many opportunities to vote for rules and laws either directly or through your elected representatives. In the previous activity, you were asked to evaluate some rules and think about how to improve them. In doing so, you made a list of characteristics or features a good rule should have. Your list may have included some of the following characteristics. A good rule should be

• fair

• easy to understand

• well designed to achieve its purpose

• clear as to what is expected

• designed so that it doesn't interfere unnecessarily with other values such as privacy or freedom

• possible to follow

When you evaluate a rule or law it is useful to consider whether it has these characteristics. That is, asking whether a rule or a law has these characteristics is one of the intellectual tools you can use to evaluate the rule or the law. Other intellectual tools you can use to evaluate rules and laws are printed in the chart on page 106.

Critical Thinking Exercise

EVALUATING A LAW

You have learned some important tools for evaluating rules and laws. The following activity gives you an opportunity to use these tools. Working in small groups, read the story and answer the questions in the Intellectual Tool Chart on the next page. Be prepared to share your answers with the class.

如何评估一项规则?

作为民主国家的公民,无论是自己亲自参与还是通过普选的代表,你们将有很多机会对规则和法律进行投票。在之前的练习里,你们已经评估了某些规则,思考如何改善它们,也列出了关于一个好的规则应当具备的特性或特征的清单。你们的清单中可能包括以下一些特性。一个好的规则应当是:

- 公平的
- 易于理解的
- 经过精心设计以实现一定目标的
- 预期目标明确清晰
- 设计完善,不会干预其他例如隐私或自由等价值
- 可以遵循的

当评估某项规则或法律时,思考它是否具备这些特性会很有帮助。也就是说,质疑一项规则或法律是否具备这些特性,是一种用来评估规则或法律的知识工具。其他用来评估规则和法律的知识工具,可以在第 107 页的图表中找到。

重点思考练习

评估一项法律

之前你们已经学会了某些评估规则和法律的重要工具,下面你们将有机会运用这些工具。分成小组阅读以下案例,并回答知识工具图表中的问题。准备好与全班分享你的答案。

The Amplified Car Stereo Law

As technology has advanced, companies have developed super-amplified car stereo systems that can blast music at ear-splitting levels. Frequently drivers with these stereo systems play them at full volume and the noise often distracts other drivers. To combat this problem, the governor signed a law that makes it illegal to operate a sound system in a vehicle if the sound can be heard more than fifty feet away. Offenders are subject to a $50 fine for the first violation and higher fines for later offenses.

Reaction to the new law has varied. Police and sheriff's departments support the measure, claiming that issuing a citation and a fine will deter the high-volume sound abuse. Manufacturers of the high-powered stereo systems oppose the law, arguing that education would be a better deterrent.

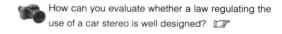 How can you evaluate whether a law regulating the use of a car stereo is well designed? ☞

Using the Lesson

1. Think of a problem at your school. Develop a rule with a group of your classmates to help deal with that problem. Present the problem and your rule to the rest of the class. Discuss your rule using the procedure for evaluating rules you just learned.

2. Look at newspaper or magazine articles and find one about a rule that interests you. It can be in government, business, sports, or another area. Evaluate this rule using the intellectual tools you have learned and write an editorial supporting your position.

扩增汽车音响法

随着技术的进步，许多公司已经研发出超级扩增汽车音响系统，使汽车音乐爆发出震耳欲聋的效果。通常安装这些音响系统的司机都喜欢把音量开到最大，所产生的噪音也往往影响到其他驾驶人。为了解决这一问题，州长签署了一项法律，规定若在离车 50 英尺以外的地方还能听到这辆车的音响声，则被视为违法。违例者初犯将被罚款 50 美元，累犯次数越多，罚款越多。

新的法律出台后，各方反应不一。警察部门都支持该项措施，他们认为开传单和罚款都将消除大音量的声音污染。高功率立体声音响系统的制造商们则反对这项法律，认为教育是比罚款更好的威慑力量。

针对一项规范汽车音响使用的法律，你如何评估这项法律是否经过了精心设计？

知识运用

1. 试想一个你所在学校的问题。和同学们组成小组来制定一项有助于解决这一问题的规则。向班里其他同学描述你们提出的问题和制定的规则。运用刚刚学到的评估规则的程序来进行讨论。

2. 浏览报纸或杂志上的文章，寻找一个感兴趣的规则，这个规则可以是政府的、企业的、体育界的或其他领域的。运用本课学到的知识工具，评估这项规则，并写一篇评论来支持自己的观点。

Intellectual Tool Chart for Evaluating Rules and Laws	
Questions	**Answers**
1. What is the rule to be evaluated?	
2. What is the purpose of the rule?	
3. Is a rule necessary or are there better ways to accomplish the same purpose?	
4. What might be the effects of the rule?	
5. What are the strengths and weaknesses of the rule? Is the rule • fair • easy to understand • well designed to achieve its purpose • clear as to what is expected • designed so that it doesn't interfere unnecessarily with other values such as privacy or freedom • possible to follow	
6. What do you think? Should the rule be kept as it is, changed, or eliminated? Why?	

评估规则和法律的知识工具表	
问题	答案
1.要评估的规则是什么？	
2.该规则的目标是什么？	
3.为实现这一目标，该规则是必需的吗？ 　还有没有更好的方法？	
4.该规则可能产生的影响是什么？	
5.这项规则的优势和劣势是什么？ 　这项规则是否是： 　・公平的 　・易于理解的 　・精心设计以实现一定目标的 　・清楚预期是什么 　・是经过设计的，使它不要干预其他价值 　　例如隐私或自由 　・可以遵循的	
6.你怎么看？这项规则应当保持现状？ 　被改变？还是被取消？为什么？	

LESSON 7
How Would You Create a Law?

Purpose of Lesson

In this lesson you take part in a simulated debate in the United States Senate. You consider a problem that is before the Senate, help develop a bill to solve this problem, and try to convince other senators that your bill is the best solution. When you have completed this lesson you should be able to explain and defend the position you have taken.

Terms to Know

extinct
endangered species
wildlife preservation

Critical Thinking Exercise
CREATING AND DEFENDING A LAW

Imagine that you are a member of the United States Senate. You learn that various species of fish, wildlife, and plants have become extinct in the United States. In addition, the populations of certain other species have become so diminished that it is likely they also will become extinct if action is not taken quickly.

 How can you decide whether a law protecting endangered species such as the spotted owl is a good law? ☞

第七课：如何制定一项法律？

本课目标

　　在这一课中，你们将参加一次美国参议院的模拟辩论。在此之前先思考并提出一个问题，然后制定一项法案来解决这个问题，并试图说服其他参议员相信你们的提案是最好的解决方法。学完本课后，你们应当能够解释和论证自己的观点。

掌握词汇

　　灭绝　　濒危物种　　野生动物保护

重点思考练习

制定一项法律并为之辩护

　　假设你是美国参议院的一位议员，最近你了解到在美国许多种类的鱼、野生动物和植物正濒临灭绝。此外，其他物种的数量也在急剧减少，如果不立即采取行动，很可能也将很快消失。

如何判断一部保护濒危物种（例如花斑猫头鹰）的法律是好的法律？

This situation has occurred for several reasons. First, there have not been adequate laws to protect the endangered species. Second, urban industrial growth has taken place without adequate protection of plants, fish, and wildlife. Third, the use of dangerous pesticides in agriculture has destroyed certain plants and animals.

You and the other members of Congress have the duty and power to make new laws. A colleague has introduced a bill that might help protect endangered species. This bill, called the Federal Endangered Species Act, provides a program for the conservation of endangered species of fish, wildlife, and plants in the particular locations where they live and grow.

With regard to the animals specified in this bill, it would become a federal crime to do the following:

- import any such species into, or export any such species out of, the United States
- own, deliver, carry, transport, or ship by any means any such species
- sell or offer for sale any such species

The bill would impose a $10,000 fine on any person who knowingly violates its provisions.

Evaluating the Endangered Species Law

Read the questions below and share your answers with the rest of the class.

1. What proposed law is to be evaluated?

2. What is the purpose of the proposed law?

3. Is a law necessary or are there better ways to achieve the purpose?

4. What do you think would be some effects of the proposed law?

5. What are the strengths and weaknesses of the proposed law?

6. Do you think the proposed law should be kept as it is, changed, or eliminated? Why?

这种情况的发生有以下几点原因：首先，没有足够的法律来保护濒危物种；其次，城市工业增长过快的同时却没有合理保护植物、鱼类和野生动物；第三，农业中使用的有毒杀虫剂毁灭了某些植物和动物。

你和国会其他议员有责任和权力制定新的法律。有一位议员提出了一项可能有助于保护濒临灭绝物种的法案——"联邦濒危物种法案"，为生长在特定地域的鱼类、野生动植物的濒危物种制定了一项保护计划（任何针对该法案当中规定的动物做出以下行为，则将被联邦法律视为犯罪）。

- 将任何此类物种进口或出口美国
- 以任何方式拥有、交付、携带、运输或运送任何此类物种
- 出售或约定出售任何此类物种

该法案将对任何故意违反其条款的人罚款一万美元。

评估濒危物种法案

阅读下列问题，并与班上其他同学分享你的答案。

1. 要评估的法律草案是什么？
2. 该法律草案的目标是什么？
3. 为实现这个目标，该项法律是必需的吗？还有没有其他更好的方法？
4. 你认为这项法律草案可能产生哪些影响？
5. 该法律草案有什么优势和劣势？
6. 你认为这项法律草案应当保持现状？还是要改变？或是被取消？为什么？

Positions of Senatorial Groups

The bill has been referred to the Senate Committee on Environment and Public Works. Your teacher will divide your class into the following three groups of senators on the committee. Each group will take a different position on how to solve the endangered species problem.

Group 1: Senators who believe the national government has a major responsibility

You believe that the federal government should take a major role in helping to solve the problem of endangered species. You think the national government should set general policies and provide funds, and local governments should have to help with the federal programs. You also think that educational institutions should teach methods of saving our wildlife. You are willing to reduce other parts of the budget to pay for the endangered species program.

Group 2: Senators who believe the national government has a limited responsibility

You think that the federal government should not take the main responsibility for dealing with the problem of endangered species. You believe that each state should maintain its own ecological balance and that we should spend tax. money on more urgently needed programs than wildlife conservation. You also recognize that hunting and fishing bring considerable income to certain states. You believe that federal government policies concerning wildlife preservation hurt those states that depend on income from hunting and fishing.

 What arguments should members ofCongress consider in deciding whether to support aproposed law? ☞

参议院小组的观点

现在该法案已经被提交到参议院环境和公共工程委员会。老师将会把你们班分成以下三个小组，相当于委员会里的三组议员。针对如何解决濒危物种问题，每个小组将各自持有不同观点。

第一组：认为国家和政府应当承担主要责任的参议员

你们认为联邦政府应当在帮助解决濒危物种问题当中发挥关键作用。你们认为国家应该制定基本政策并提供资金，而地方政府应协助联邦政府的方案。你们也主张教育机构应该教授人们拯救野生动物的方法。你们同意削减其他部分的政府预算，用于支持濒危物种的保护方案。

第二组：认为国家和政府责任有限的参议员

你们认为联邦政府不应该在解决濒危物种问题方面负主要责任。你们提出，各州应维持自身的生态平衡。同时各州应当把税款花在更迫切急需投资的地方，而不是野生动物保护方案。你们承认狩猎和渔业为某些州带来了可观的收入。你们认为联邦政府关于野生动物保护的政策损害了这些依赖狩猎和捕鱼收入的各州的利益。

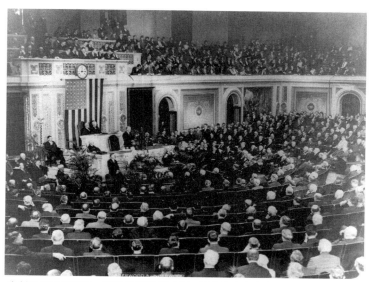

在判断是否要支持一项法律草案的时候，国会议员应当考虑什么依据？

Group 3: Senators who favor a compromise

You agree with parts of the other two groups' positions. You think the states should protect their wildlife. On the other hand, you believe that the federal government should play a more active role. For example, you believe that we need federal laws to prevent the sale of wild animal products (such as fur coats) that require the death of the animal. You also think that both the federal and state governments should share the responsibility and the cost of protecting wildlife.

Developing a Bill

Each group should begin by selecting a spokesperson and a recorder. Then each group should develop an alternative bill that represents its position on how to solve the problem of endangered species. You should evaluate the alternative you proposed by answering the following questions:

• What is the purpose of your alternative bill?

• Do you think there are better ways than making a law to achieve the purpose? Explain.

• What effects would your bill have if it became law?

• What are the strengths and weaknesses of your bill?

• Why should the senators pass your bill?

Directions for a Senate Debate

1. The class should select a person to serve as chairman of the Senate Committee on Environment and Public Works who will chair the proceedings.

2. Each group will have three minutes to present its bill to the committee. After each presentation, other senators may question or criticize the bill presented. Members of the group creating the bill may respond to these criticisms.

3. Each group may amend its bill if necessary to win votes or they may develop and present a compromise bill.

第三组：赞成妥协的参议员

你们部分同意以上两组的观点。一方面你们认为各州应该保护自己的野生动物，另一方面，你们认为联邦政府应该发挥更积极的作用。例如，你们主张需要制定联邦法律来阻止出售危害动物生命的野生动物产品（如毛皮大衣）。你们也认为，无论是联邦还是各州政府都应分担保护野生动物的责任和费用。

制定一项提案

首先，每个小组应选出一位发言人和一位记录员。然后，每个小组应制定一项备选法案，用来阐述各组关于如何解决濒危物种问题的观点。你们应当通过以下问题来评估自己提出的备选法案：

- 你们提出的备选法案的目标是什么？
- 除了制定法律以外，还有更好的方法实现上述目标吗？请解释。
- 如果你们的提案获得通过成为法律，将产生什么效果？
- 你们的提案有什么优势和劣势？
- 为什么参议员们应当批准你们的提案？

模拟参议院辩论指导

1. 全班应当选出一位同学，扮演参议院环境与公共工程委员会主席，他将主持辩论大会。

2. 每个小组将有3分钟时间向委员会陈述自己的提案。每次发言结束后，其他参议员可以针对该提案提出质疑或批评。制定提案的小组成员可以对这些评论做出回应。

3. 为了赢得选票，每个小组可以修改自己的提案，也可以制订并提出一个折衷方案。

4. After completing the debate, the committee should vote on the bills before it. When voting, consider the following questions:

- What is the purpose of each bill?

- What would be the effects of each bill if it were passed?

- What are the strengths and weaknesses of each bill?

Using the Lesson

1. Did you agree with the class decision? Why or why not? Write a short essay in your journal describing your reaction to the Senate committee debate and vote. Discuss your views on what type of law would best deal with the problem of endangered species.

2. Choose a bill that is before your state legislature or Congress. Evaluate the proposed legislation using the criteria in this lesson. Write a letter to your representative urging him or her to support your position on the bill.

4. 辩论结束后，委员会应当那个对提案进行表决。投票时，请考虑以下问题：

- 每项提案的目标是什么？
- 如果某项提案获得通过，将会产生怎样的影响？
- 每项提案有有什么优势和劣势？

知识运用

1. 你是否同意全班的最后决定？为什么？为什么不？在你的笔记上写一篇短文，描述你对参议院委员会辩论和投票的看法，探讨你认为哪种法律是处理濒危物种问题最好的法案。

2. 选择一项你们州议会或国会提出的法案，按照本课中所学到的标准，评估这一法律提案。给你们州的议员写一封信，请他或她支持你关于该提案的观点。

Unit Four

What Are the Benefits and Costs of Authority?

> ### Purpose of Unit
>
> Every use of authority has certain results. For example, when U.S. troops are sent overseas as part of a United Nations force, the results may include restoring peace or assisting refugees in a troubled part of the world. Other results, however, might include the death of some civilians and military service members, the destruction of public facilities, and financial costs to U.S. taxpayers. We need to decide whether the benefits (advantages) of a particular use of authority outweigh the costs (disadvantages) for us as individuals and for society.

In this unit you will learn some of the common benefits and costs of authority. You also will learn some intellectual tools to use in evaluating positions and institutions which have authority. These tools will help you decide whether the duties, powers, privileges, and limitations of a position or an institution have been well planned, or if they need to be changed. You also will have the opportunity to use these tools to design a position of authority.

第四单元：权威有哪些利弊得失？

单元目标

权威的每一次运用都会产生某些特定的结果。例如，当美军作为联合国部队的一部分向海外派兵时，其结果包括：使世界上某个动荡不安地区恢复和平或帮助难民。然而结果还可能包括：一些平民和军方人员的死亡、公共设施的破坏、美国纳税人的财政开支增加。我们需要判断权威的某种特定用途所带来的利益（优势）是否大于作为个人的我们和社会的损失（劣势）。

在这个单元里，你们将学到权威带来的常见利弊得失，也会学到评估权威职位和机构的知识工具。这些工具将有助于判断某个职位和机构的职责、权力、特权和限制是否经过周密的计划，或者是否需要改变。你们也将有机会运用这些知识工具来设计一种权威职位。

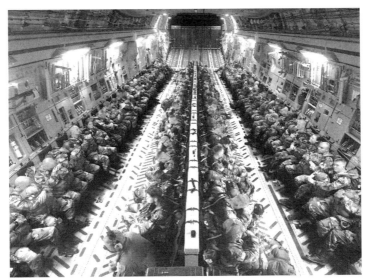

 What might be some consequences of a government decision to exercise authority by sending troops to maintain peace in another part of the world? Which of these consequences would be benefits, which would be costs?

一个国家的政府决定通过派遣军队到世界另一个地方维持和平来达到行使权威的目的，这一举动可能产生哪些后果？这些结果中哪些是利益（好处），哪些将是行动的弊病（损失）？

LESSON 8
What Are Some Consequences of Authority?

Purpose of Lesson

In this lesson you will identify consequences of the use of authority. You will classify these consequences as benefits or costs. When you have completed the lesson, you should be able to explain some common benefits and costs of authority. You also should be able to use these ideas in evaluating and taking positions on issues of authority.

Terms to Know

efficiency	accountability
vigilance	inaccessibility
economic costs	incompetence

What are the benefits and costs of authority?

To begin thinking about the consequences of authority, we will look at a hypothetical situation. Suppose that the number of automobile accidents among teenage drivers has increased sharply. To reduce the number of such accidents, the state legislature passed a law stating that no one under the age of twenty-one could get a driver's license.

• What might be some consequences of such a law?

• Which of these consequences would be benefits? Which would be costs?

• How do you think the various people affected by this law-teenagers, their parents, the police, the state legislators-would feel about the benefits and costs involved?

第八课：权威会产生哪些结果？

> ### 本课目标
>
> 在这一课中，你们会了解到行使权威的结果，这些结果可以被归类为利益（好处）或弊病（损失）。学完本课后，你们应该能够解释行使权威通常产生的利弊得失。你们也应该能够运用这些观念来评估权威并提出自己的看法。

掌握词汇

效率	难以接近
问责	经济成本
警觉	无能

什么是权威的利弊得失？

首先，为思考权威产生的结果，我们将首先进行假设：假设未成年人驾车所导致的车祸急剧增加，为了减少这类事故，州议会通过了一项法律，规定 21 岁以上公民才可以领取驾驶执照。

- 这样一项法规可能产生哪些结果？
- 哪些结果是利益（好处）？哪些是弊病（损失）？
- 你觉得受这项法规影响的未成年人、他们的父母、警察和州议员，他们对这项法规的利弊得失会怎么看？

Critical Thinking Exercise

DECIDING WHETHER A CONSEQUENCE IS A BENEFIT OR COST

In this activity you will work with a study partner to discuss some benefits and costs of using authority. Read the following situations and answer the "What do you think?" questions. Be prepared to share your answers with the rest of the class.

- To combat an increase in juvenile crime, the city council passed a law imposing a 10:30 p.m. curfew on people under the age of eighteen.

- To control pollution, Congress passed a law that set high standards for waste disposal from industrial plants. Any factory that did not follow these standards within six months would receive heavy fines.

- To reduce violence, the state legislature passed a law that made it a crime to print or sell books or magazines that showed or described acts of violence.

What do you think?

1. What might be some consequences of authority in each situation?

2. Which of these consequences would be benefits?

3. Which of these consequences would be costs?

What are some common benefits and costs of authority?

When making decisions about issues of authority, it is important to identify the possible benefits and costs involved.

Benefits might include the following:

- **Security.** The use of authority may make people feel more secure by providing a predictable order and by protecting the rights of individuals and groups. For example, laws against murder, assault, drunk driving, and other offenses are uses of authority that provide security.

- **Fairness.** People can use authority to promote the fair distribution of resources and the fair management of conflicts. For example, laws protect people's rights to a hearing in court.

重点思考练习

判断结果是利益（好处）还是弊病（损失）

在本次练习中，与一位同学合作讨论行使权威带来的利弊得失。阅读以下事例，并回答"你怎么看？"部分的问题。准备好与班上其他同学分享你的答案。

- 为打击日益增多的青少年犯罪，市政厅通过了一项法律，对未满十八岁的人每晚10点30分之后实施宵禁。
- 为控制污染，国会通过一项法律，为工业厂房的废物处理设立了高标准。6个月内不达标的工厂将被施以巨额罚款。
- 为减少暴力犯罪，州议会通过了一项法律，印刷或销售有暴力行为描述的书籍或杂志将被视为犯罪。

你怎么看？

1. 以上事例中权威产生了哪些结果？
2. 其中哪些结果是利益（好处）？
3. 其中哪些结果是弊病（损失）？

行使权威有哪些常见的利弊得失？

在判断某些权威问题时，重要的是明确其中可能包含的利益（好处）和弊病（损失）。利益（好处）可能包括以下内容：

安全 通过提供一种可预测的秩序，以及通过保护个人和群体的权利，行使权威可以使人们感到更安全。例如：那些针对谋杀、伤害、酒后驾车及其他罪行的法律就是运用权威来保障人们的安全。

公平 人们可以行使权威来促进资源的公平分配，以及公平地解决冲突。例如：法律保障人民在法院聆讯的权利。

- **Freedom.** Laws such as the Bill of Rights may protect the individual's right to freedom of religion and expression.

- **Efficiency.** The clear assignment of responsibilities to various authorities may promote greater efficiency in making and carrying out decisions. For example, a principal might assign administrative tasks to several teachers to ensure the smooth operation of the school.

- **Quality of life.** Laws and the people who enforce them may protect and improve the quality of life. For example, laws may forbid the dumping of poisonous substances near water supplies.

 What might be some benefits of using authority to protect the environment? ☞

自由　像《人权法案》这样的法律可以保护个人的权利——宗教和言论自由。

效率　将责任明确划分给各种权威，可以提高制定和实施决策的效率。例如：校长可以将管理任务分配给几位老师,确保学校工作的正常运转。

生活品质　法律和执法者可以保护和改善生活质量。例如：法律可以禁止在靠近水源的地方倾倒有毒物质。

行使权威保护环境可能有哪些利益（好处）？

- **Accountability.** When we place people in positions of authority, we can hold them accountable for fulfilling the responsibilities of their jobs. For example, voters can hold the president accountable for performing the duties of his or her office as listed in the Constitution.

- **Provision of essential services.** We can provide some services we need by passing laws and appointing people to positions of authority to perform these services. For example, laws may allow hiring teachers, police officers, welfare workers, and health and safety inspectors.

Costs might include the following:

- **Misuse of power.** People filling positions of authority might misuse their positions and the power allocated to them. For example, in the Soviet Union Josef Stalin (1879-1953) abused his power by causing many of his political opponents to be murdered.

- **Need for vigilance.** We must make sure that people in positions of authority perform their responsibilities within acceptable limits. For example, citizen "watchdog" groups monitor the activities of government agencies and elected representatives.

What might be some costs of Governor George Wallace exercising authority to block integration at the University of Alabama in 1963? ☞

问责　当我们选出担任权威职位的人时，我们可以追究他们是否履行了自身的工作职责。举例来说，选民可以问责总统是否履行了宪法中列明的他或她的行政职责。

提供必要的服务　通过批准法律和选派担任权威职位的人实施服务可以提供某些我们需要的服务。例如：法律允许聘用教师、警察、福利工人和健康及安全监察员。

弊病（损失）可能包括以下内容：

权力的滥用。担任权威职位的人可能会滥用其职位和附带权力。例如，前苏联领导人约瑟夫·斯大林（1879 — 1953）滥用他的权力，导致他的许多政治对手被杀害。

需要保持警惕　我们必须确保担任权威职位的人在可接受的范围内履行其职责。例如：公民"监督团体"负责监督政府机构和民选代表的活动。

1963年州长乔治·华莱士运用权威阻止阿拉巴马大学的种族融合可能有哪些弊病（损失）？

- **Inflexibility and resistance to change.** In some instances, positions of authority can promote an unwillingness to change among those who hold these positions. This rigidity may make adjusting to new and different situations difficult. For example, many local government officials opposed the Supreme Court's school desegregation rulings.

- **Inaccessibility.** Due to the complexity and size of many large institutions, gaining access to people in specific positions of authority may be difficult. For example, a family needing affordable housing might need to visit several different government agencies to get help.

- **Limitations on freedom.** Every exercise of authority involves by definition a limitation on freedom. For example, parents' authority to set curfews for their children limits the children's freedom.

- **Economic costs.** It costs money to support people and institutions in positions of authority. For example, we pay taxes to the federal government to pay the salaries of bureaucrats, elected officials, judges, law enforcement officers, and members of the armed services.

What do you think?

1. What examples can you give from your own experience of the benefits of authority?

2. What examples can you give from your own experience of the costs of authority?

Which benefits and costs are most important?

Identifying the benefits and costs of a law is important in deciding whether to support it. However, we also must decide which benefits and costs are most important to us as individuals. For example, recall the earlier discussion of a 10:30 p.m. curfew for teenagers. Both adults and juveniles would agree that this curfew would have the cost of limiting teenagers' freedom but might also have the benefit of decreasing juvenile crime. Some might think that the benefit of decreased crime is more important than the cost of limiting the freedom of juveniles. Others might not agree, We should consider different points of view when examining the benefits and costs of authority in any given situation.

刚性和抵制变革　在某些情况下，职位的权威性使那些在位者不愿做出改变。这种僵化性很难应对不同情况和新问题做出调整。例如，许多地方政府官员反对最高法院的取消学校种族隔离的判决。

难以接近　因为很多大型机构的复杂性与规模，接近某些权威职位的人物可能会很困难。例如，一个需要住房救济的家庭可能需要去很多政府部门才能得到帮助。

对自由的限制　每一次运用权威都涉及到对自由的限制。例如，家长对子女设置门禁的权威就限制了孩子们的自由。

经济成本　支持处于权威职位的人和机构需要花费金钱。例如，我们向联邦政府纳税以便为行政官员、民选官员、法官、执法人员和武装部队成员支付工资。

你怎么看？

1. 请从你的个人经验中，举出关于权威的利益（好处）的例子。
2. 请从你的个人经验中，举出关于权威的弊病（损失）的例子。

哪些利益（好处）和弊病（损失）是最重要的？

在判断是否支持一项法律的时候，明确它的利弊得失是很重要的。但是，我们也必须判断哪些利弊得失对我们个人来说是最重要的。例如，针对之前讨论过的未成年人晚间 10 时 30 分之后的宵禁问题，成年人和未成年人都会同意该宵禁令限制了青少年的自由，但也有减少未成年人犯罪的好处。有些人可能认为减少犯罪的利益（好处）要比限制未成年人自由的弊病（损失）来得重要，其他人可能不这么看。在考察特定情况下行使权威的利弊得失时，我们应该考虑不同的观点。

Critical Thinking Exercise

TAKING A POSITION

Assume that your state legislature is considering a bill to ban the sale and possession of assault-type automatic weapons. Your teacher will divide your class into five groups to develop positions on the bill, Each group should represent one of the organizations listed below.

Each organization should make a presentation about which benefits and costs are most important from its point of view.

• Committee for a Safe Community

• Main Town Gun Owners Association

• Police Department

• Eagle Arms Weapons Factory

• Association of Principled Pacifists

What do you think?

1. What benefits and costs did each group consider most important?

2. What interests affected how each group saw the importance of the various benefits and costs?

Using the Lesson

1. What are some rules you have at school? Pick two or three of these rules and describe the benefits and costs of each,

2. Think about a television program or a movie you have seen that showed an exercise of authority. In your journal, make a list of the consequences of that exercise of authority. For each consequence, decide if it is a benefit or a cost.

重点思考练习

提出你的观点

假设你们州的议会正在考虑一项禁止销售和持有攻击型自动武器的法案。老师将你们班分成以下 5 个小组来制定该法案。每一组需要代表下列组织机构之一。针对哪些利弊得失是最重要的问题，每个组织机构都要陈述发表自己的观点。

· 某个安定社区的委员会
· 主要城区的枪支所有者协会
· 警察总署
· 鹰牌武器制造厂
· 有原则的和平主义者

你怎么看?

1. 各组认为哪些利弊得失最重要？

2. 什么利益影响了每组重视不同的利弊得失？

知识运用

1. 你在学校要遵守哪些规则？从中选出两个或三个，并描述每条规则的利弊得失。

2. 在你看过的某个电视节目或某部电影中，想想哪些反映了权威的运用。在你的笔记本上，列出这些权威运用的结果。判断每一种结果是利益（好处）还是弊病（损失）。

LESSON 9

How Can You Evaluate the Benefits and Costs of Authority?

Purpose of Lesson

In this lesson you will consider the benefits and costs of authority in a courtroom situation. After studying the situation, everyone in the class will participate in a hearing and judge the issues involved. When you have completed the lesson, you should be able to explain the usefulness of considering benefits and costs in making decisions about authority.

Terms to Know

public defender

bailiff

Critical Thinking Exercise

EVALUATING THE BENEFITS AND COSTS OF AUTHORITY

Your teacher will divide your class into three groups. One group will act as lawyers for Mr. Allen, one group will act as lawyers for the government, and one group will act as judges considering the case on appeal. To prepare for the hearing, each group should read the background of the case, consider the facts involved, and answer the three questions on benefits and costs on p. 140.

第九课：如何评估权威的利弊得失？

本课目标

　　本课中你们将思考在法庭上行使权威的利弊得失。班上每一位同学都将参加一场模拟听证会，并针对某个问题做出裁决。学完本课后，你们应当能够解释对利弊得失的考虑在裁决权威问题时的作用。

掌握词汇

　　公设辩护律师
　　法警

重点思考练习

评估权威的利弊得失

　　老师将把你们班分成 3 组。其中一组将担任艾伦先生的律师，一组将作为政府的律师出庭，最后一组将作为法官对这起上诉案件做出判决。在准备听证会的过程中，每组应当仔细阅读案件的背景，思考案件涉及的事实，并回答第 141 页中有关利弊得失的三个问题。

Illinois v. Allen

On August 12, 1956, William Allen walked into a tavern and took $200 from the bartender at gunpoint Later that day, police arrested Allen. The bartender identified him as the robber.

Since he could not afford to hire his own attorney, the court offered Allen a choice between the public defender or an attorney from the Bar Association Defense Committee. Allen refused both. He asked to represent himself. The judge told Allen, "I'll let you be your own lawyer, but I'll ask Mr. Kelly (a court-appointed lawyer) to sit in and protect your rights."

The trial began on September 9, 1957. Allen questioned the first potential juror at great length. Finally, the trial judge interrupted. He told Allen to ask questions only about the person's qualifications. At that point Allen began to argue with the judge in a very disrespectful way.

Then the judge asked Kelly to continue examining the jurors. Allen continued to talk, saying that Kelly was not going to act as his lawyer. He said to the judge, "When I go for lunch, you're going to be a corpse here." Then Allen tore up his attorney's files and threw the papers on the floor.

The trial judge said, "One more outbreak of that sort and I'll remove you from the courtroom." Allen ignored the warning.

 What might be some consequences when a judge orders an unruly defendant removed from the courtroom? Which consequences would be benefits, which would be costs? ☞

伊利诺伊州诉艾伦案

1956 年 8 月 12 日，威廉·艾伦走进一家酒馆，并用枪指着酒保，抢走了 200 美元。当天晚些时候，警方逮捕了艾伦。酒保指认他为劫匪。

由于他没有钱为自己聘请律师，法庭让艾伦选择一位公设辩护律师或者一位来自律师协会的辩护律师。艾伦拒绝了，他要求自辩。法官告诉艾伦："我会允许你为自己辩护，但我会请凯利先生（法庭指定的律师）列席听证并保护你的权利。"

1957 年 9 月 9 日，案件开庭。艾伦花了很长时间质疑第一位候选陪审员，直到主审法官打断他。法官告诉艾伦，他只能询问与个人资格有关的问题，艾伦随即开始在这一点上非常无礼地与法官争辩。

随后法官请凯利先生继续审查陪审员。艾伦接着说他认为凯利不打算做他的律师。他跟法官说："当我去吃午饭的时候，你会变成这里的一具尸体。"接着艾伦将他的律师的所有文件撕烂并扔在地上。

主审法官说："如果再有一次这样的举动，我将把你驱逐出法庭。"艾伦对警告置若罔闻。

法官宣布将一名不守规矩的被告逐出法庭会产生哪些结果？哪些结果是利益（好处），哪些将是弊病（损失）？

'There's not going to be no trial," Allen said. "You can bring your shackles and straitjacket and put them on me and tape my mouth, but it will do no good because there's not going to be no trial."

The judge ordered the court officers to remove Allen from the courtroom. The jury was selected without Allen present. Later, when the jury was not present, the judge brought Allen into the courtroom. Allen said that he wanted to be in the courtroom during his trial. The judge said that he would permit Allen to remain if he did not interfere with the presentation of the case.

The jury came in and sat down. Allen stood up and said, 'There is going to be no proceeding. I'm going to start talking and I'm going to keep on talking all through the trial." The trial judge again ordered the bailiff to remove Allen from the courtroom.

After this second removal, Allen remained out of the courtroom except when they brought him in for witnesses to identify. During one of these appearances, Allen used obscene language to the judge. After the prosecution presented its case, the judge again told Allen that he could return to the courtroom whenever he agreed to conduct himself properly. Allen promised that he would conduct himself properly, but due to the way he had behaved, the court officers bound and gagged him during the presentation of his defense.

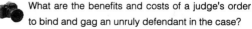 What are the benefits and costs of a judge's order to bind and gag an unruly defendant in the case?
☞

　　"审判不可能不继续"，艾伦说："你可以把你的锁链和囚衣拿来绑住我，把我的嘴巴封上，但这完全没有任何好处，因为你不可能不继续审判。"

　　法官下令法警将艾伦带出法庭，并在艾伦不出庭的情况下选出了陪审团。然后，在陪审团不在场时，法官再次提请艾伦出庭。艾伦说，他希望审判期间一直待在法庭。法官同意并允许艾伦在场，前提是他不干预案件陈述过程。

　　陪审团走进法庭并坐了下来。艾伦站起来说："这里根本就没有什么诉讼程序。我要开始发言了，我要在审判过程中一直说话。"主审法官再次命令法警将艾伦带出法庭。

　　第二次被逐出法庭后，除了法警带他到法庭给证人辨认以外，艾伦一直待在庭外。某一次出庭时，艾伦还用淫秽语言攻击了法官。当控方介绍完案情后，法官再次通知艾伦，只要他行为适当就可以回到法庭，艾伦对此承诺发誓。但介于他之前的行为表现，在他的辩护陈述阶段，法警将他绑起来并塞住了他的嘴。

法官下令将被告绑起来并塞住被告的嘴，会有什么利弊得失？

The jury found Allen guilty of armed robbery. He was sentenced to ten to thirty years in prison.

Allen appealed his conviction, and his case eventually reached the Supreme Court of the United States. Allen claimed that the trial judge had conducted the trial unfairly and had deprived him of rights guaranteed by the Sixth Amendment of the Constitution. Specifically, Allen claimed that the Constitution gave him the right to be present at his own trial and to act as his own lawyer. He also argued that his trial was fundamentally unfair because he was bound and gagged during the presentation of his defense.

What do you think?

1. What might be the consequences of the trial judge's exercise of authority in this case? Consider the judge's decisions

• to require Allen to be represented by an attorney

• to remove Allen from the courtroom

• to require Allen to be bound and gagged during the presentation of his defense

2. Which consequences are costs?

3. Which consequences are benefits?

Preparation for the Hearings

Consider the following question: In view of the benefits and costs involved, was the trial judge justified in requiring an attorney to represent Allen; in ordering Allen's removal from the courtroom; in ordering Allen to be bound and gagged during the presentation of his defense?

Group 1: You represent lawyers for the government.

Group 2: You represent lawyers for Mr. Allen.

Group 3: You represent judges hearing the case on appeal.

Each group should discuss the issues from their assigned point of view and prepare arguments to present before the judges. Judges should review the case and prepare questions to ask each side.

陪审团判定艾伦犯有持械抢劫罪，他被判处 10 到 30 年徒刑。

艾伦不服判决，并提起上诉，他的案子最终提交到美国最高法院。艾伦声称，主审法官对他进行了不公平的审判，剥夺了宪法第六修正案所保障的他的权利。具体地说，艾伦认为宪法赋予了他出席自己的审判并为自己辩护的权利。他还认为，他的审判根本就是不公平的，因为在他的辩护陈述阶段，他被绑住了并且还被塞住了嘴。

你怎么看？

1. 在这个案例里，主审法官行使权威产生了什么的结果？考虑法官的决定：
   - 要求艾伦必须由律师代表出庭；
   - 将艾伦逐出法庭；
   - 要求艾伦在他的辩论陈述阶段被绑起来并被塞住嘴巴。
2. 其中哪些结果是弊病（损失）？
3. 其中哪些结果是利益（好处）？

准备听证会

思考以下问题：考虑到案例中涉及的利弊得失，主审法官要求律师代表艾伦出庭是正当的吗？下令将艾伦逐出法庭是正当的吗？命令艾伦在他的辩护陈述阶段被绑起来并被塞住嘴巴是正当的吗？

第一组：代表政府的律师

第二组：代表艾伦的律师

第三组：代表审理该上诉案件的法官

每个小组应当从各自被分配的观点角度来讨论问题，同时要准备提交给法官的证据。主审法官应当全面考察这个案件，并准备要问各组的问题。

Procedures for the Appeal Hearings

1. After the preparation period, the class will be divided into "triads"-or small groups of three students. Each triad will consist of a judge, a lawyer for Mr. Allen, and a lawyer for the government.

2. The judge will call the hearing to order. Each side will have six minutes to present its arguments. The lawyer for Mr. Allen should go first. During the arguments, the judge may interrupt to ask questions.

After each side has presented its arguments and been questioned by the judge, a two-minute rebuttal may be presented by each side. Again, the lawyer for Mr. Allen should go first. Finally, the judge should make his or her decision and explain the reasoning that supports it.

3. The class as a whole should then discuss the case. Begin the discussion by having judges report their decisions to the class as a whole. Did all the judges reach the same conclusion? Which arguments were perceived to be the strongest? Finally, the class should discuss the process that was used in the triads, which is similar to the process actually used in an appellate court. Is it fair? Why or why not? What changes would you suggest to make it better?

Using the Lesson

1. Write a letter to the editor supporting or opposing the position taken by the judges. Defend your position in terms of the benefits and costs involved in the case.

2. Interview someone who is in a position of authority (school principal, police officer, city official, etc.). Ask this person to describe some of the benefits and costs of his or her exercise of authority. Then interview someone who this person's authority affects (student, citizen, or resident of the city). Ask this person to describe some of the benefits and costs of the exercise of authority. Compare your two lists of benefits and costs. Write a report describing the similarities and differences.

上诉听证会的流程

1. 准备阶段之后，全班将被分成若干"三人小组"（每三名学生组成一个小组）。每个三人小组都将包括一名法官、艾伦先生的律师以及一位政府的律师。

2. 法官将宣布听证会开始。每一方将有 6 分钟时间陈述其论据。艾伦先生的律师应当首先进行陈述。在陈述中，法官可以打断发言并提问。

   各方都陈述完毕并回答完法官的问题后，每方还有 2 分钟的反驳辩论时间。同样，艾伦先生的律师先发言。最后，法官应做出他或她的决定，并说明理由。

3. 全班一起讨论这个案例。首先是各位法官向全班报告自己的判决。那么，是否所有的法官都得出了同样的结论？哪些论据被认为是最充分的？最后，全班一起讨论本次练习中所使用的"三人小组"流程（与现实的上诉法庭所使用的流程类似），这是否公平？为什么？为什么不？对改善这一流程你有什么建议？

知识运用

1. 写封信给编辑，要么支持，要么反对法官的观点。根据本案中所包含的利弊得失来为你的观点辩护。
2. 采访某些处于权威职位的人（例如：学校校长、警察、城市公务员等），请他们描述自己行使权威的利弊得失。然后采访那些受到这位采访对象权威影响的人（例如：学生、公民或城市居民等），请他们描述自己所受到的权威带来的利弊得失。将两组利弊得失列出清单，并进行对比。写一份报告来具体说明它们之间的相同和不同之处。

Unit Five:

What Should Be the Scope and Limits of Authority?

Purpose of Unit

Some of the most important issues we face as citizens involve questions about the scope (extent) and limits of authority. Is a particular position of authority well designed? Does it give enough power to the person in charge while establishing effective limits to prevent abuse of that power?

In this unit you will learn some ways to evaluate positions of authority. You will decide if the duties, powers, privileges, and limitations of a position of authority have been well planned or if they should be changed Finally you will put into practice what you have been studying. You will design a position of authority.

第五单元：权威的范围和限制应该是什么？

单元目标

　　我们作为公民所面临的一些最重要的问题当中包括了权威的范围（程度）和限制。某个特定的权威职位是否经过精心设计？是否在给予担任该职位的人足够的权力的同时，也建立了有效的限制防止权力的滥用？

　　在本单元，你们将学习一些方法来评估权威职位。你们将学会判断某个权威职位的职责、权力、特权和限制是否经过周密的安排，或者是否需要改变它们。最后，你们会将本课开始以来所学的知识付诸实践。你们将有机会设计一种权威职位。

 What might be the proper scope and limits of authority of a president, such as Harry Truman, and a commander in the field, such as General Douglas MacArthur during World War II?

像哈里·杜鲁门这样的总统，他的权威范围和限制可能是什么？像二战时期的道格拉斯·麦克阿瑟将军这样的军队统帅，他的权威范围和限制可能是什么？

LESSON 10

What Makes a Well-Designed Position of Authority?

Purpose of Lesson

This lesson introduces you to a set of intellectual tools useful in evaluating both positions of authority and institutions that have authority. When you have completed the lesson, you should be able to use these tools in evaluating and suggesting improvements for positions of authority.

Terms to Know

scope

limits

humane

What makes a position of authority well designed?

By now you must have realized that people in positions of authority affect you in important ways every day. Parents, teachers, and school officials make decisions and take actions that can influence your life. Our local, state, and federal governments are run largely by people in positions of authority. These include such diverse positions as crossing guard, police officer, judge, member of Congress, and president. We, the people of the United States, have given great responsibilities and powers to many of these people. We hope that these powers will make them able to provide us with the services we want and need.

Some of the most important issues we face as citizens involve questions about the positions of authority in our system.

People have different opinions about whether some positions of authority are well designed. People have different opinions about whether certain positions have too much or too little authority.

第十课：什么构成了一个精心设计的权威职位?

本课目标

　　本课将向你们介绍一组有助于评估权威职位和权威机构的知识工具。学完本课后，你们应该能够运用这些知识工具来评估权威职位，并提出改进建议。

掌握词汇

范围　　　　限制　　　　人道

什么构成了一个精心设计的权威地位?

　　到目前为止，你们一定已经意识到，担任权威职位的人每天都通过某种重要的方式影响着你们。家长、老师和学校的教官们作出的决定和采取的行动都可以影响你们的生活。本地、各州和联邦的政府机构基本都要依赖担任权威职位的人们来运行。这些职位非常多种多样，例如：交通协管员、警官、法官、国会议员和总统。我们美国人民赋予了这些人以相当大的责任和权力，并希望这些权力会使他们能提供我们所希望和需要的服务。

　　有关我们的政府体系中的权威职位问题，是我们作为公民所面对的最重要的问题之一。

　　对某些权威职位是否经过了精心设计，人们各有不同看法；对某些职位拥有的权威是过多还是过少，人们也持有不同的意见。

One thing is certain. Because people in positions of authority affect our lives so much, it is important to plan and evaluate what their duties, powers, privileges, and limitations should be. If we fail to consider how positions of authority are designed, it can lead to consequences that could threaten the basic freedoms on which our nation was founded.

- What historical or contemporary examples can you give of positions of authority that were poorly designed? What were the flaws in these positions of authority? What were the consequences of these flaws?

- Why might it be important to evaluate positions of authority?

Critical Thinking Exercise

EVALUATING ERRORS IN DESIGNING A POSITION OF AUTHORITY

The list below describes several positions of authority. Each position has something wrong with it. Read the list and answer the questions that follow.

1. The constitution of the state of Confusion said that the governor had to make all the laws, deliver the mail, sweep the streets, patrol for stray animals, preside over all criminal trials, and run the television station.

 Do you think the governor of the State of Confusion has too much or too little authority? ☞

　　有一点是肯定的：因为担任权威职位的人给我们的生活带来如此大的影响，规划和评估他们应有的职责、权力、特权和限制就变得非常重要。如果我们不去考虑权威职位如何设计的问题，可能导致我们国家得以建立的根本自由受到威胁。

　　在历史上或当今社会中，你能否举出经过不合理的权威职位的范例？这些权威职位的缺陷是什么？这些缺陷导致了什么结果？

　　为什么评估权威职位是很重要的？

重点思考练习

评估权威职位设计中的错误

　　阅读以下几种权威职位的描述，其中每个职位都存在一定的问题。回答材料后的问题。

1. "迷糊"州的宪法认为，州长必须制定所有法律、递送邮件、清扫街道、巡街寻找流浪动物、审判所有刑事案件并运行所有电视台。

你认为"迷糊"州的州长拥有的权威太多还是太少？

2. In the state of Perpetua, all members of the legislature were appointed for life. They could not be removed from office no matter what they did.

3. When Leroy Hawkins was appointed Boot City High's monitor by the principal, she gave him complete authority over students in the halls. She said he could make them do anything he wanted.

4. The newly elected mayor of Agoraphobia City would not allow any citizen to speak to him or write him letters. While he was mayor, he locked himself in his office and took the phone off the hook.

5. The city council hired six traffic control officers to enforce the speeding laws. It did not give the officers any police cars, motorcycles, or whistles.

6. The Grand Inquisitor was like a judge. His job was to determine guilt or innocence. He often tortured those accused of crimes to force confessions out of them. Innocent people confessed just to escape the pains of torture.

What do you think?

1. What is wrong with each position of authority described above?

2. Look at each weakness you identified. What do these weaknesses suggest about what to include in a well-designed position of authority?

How should we determine the scope and limits of authority?

The preceding activity should give you some insight into what can go wrong if a position of authority is designed badly. How can we prevent such problems? Below are eight questions-intellectual tools-you can use to evaluate the scope and limits of a particular position of authority. Work with a study partner or in small groups to review the intellectual tools and to answer the what do you think questions. Be prepared to share your answers with the class.

1. What is the position to be evaluated?

2. What is the purpose or purposes of the position?

3. Is the position necessary to accomplish these purposes?

4. What are the duties, powers, privileges, and limitations of the position?

5. What are some of the probable effects of the position as it is now designed?

2. 在佩尔佩图阿州，所有议会成员都是终身任职。无论他们做了什么都不会被免职。

3. 当勒罗伊·霍金斯被布特市立高中的校长任命为该校学监时，校长给了他管理学校所有学生的全部权威。校长说他可以让学生们做任何他要求的事。

4. "恐慌"市新当选的市长不允许任何公民跟他说话或给他写信。虽然他是市长，但他把自己锁在办公室里，并拔掉了电话线。

5. 市政厅聘请了 6 名交通协管员来监管超速法，但却没有给任何警务人员配备警车、摩托车或口哨。

6. 最高检察长就像一个法官，他的工作就是判定有罪或无罪。他经常折磨那些被指控的嫌犯，迫使他们招供。为了躲避被折磨的痛苦，无辜的人也只能认罪。

你怎么看?

1. 上述权威职位的描述中各有什么错误?

2. 观察你找出的上述缺点，这为一个精心设计的权威职位所应当包含的内容提出了什么建议?

应当如何明确权威的范围和权限?

经过以上内容的学习，你们应该已经知道如果权威职位设计不当会产生什么问题。怎样才能防止这些问题的出现?以下有 8 个问题（即一组知识工具），可以用来评估某个特定权威职位的范围和限制。与一位同学或和一个小组一起，仔细研究这组知识工具，并回答"你怎么看?"部分的问题。准备与全班分享你们的答案。

1. 要评估的职位是什么?

2. 该职位有什么目标（一个或多个）?

3. 对实现这些目标来说，该职位是否必要?

4. 该职位的责任、权力、特权和限制是什么?

5. 这个如此设计的职位可能产生哪些影响?

6. What are the strengths and weaknesses of the position?

• Is it well designed to achieve its purposes?

• Does it have enough power-adequate but not excessive?

• Are there ways to hold people in the position accountable for what they do?

• Is the position overburdened with duties?

• Are sufficient resources available to accomplish the duties of the position?

• Is there a reasonable degree of public access and input?

• Must the position use fair and humane procedures in the exercise of its powers?

• Is the position designed to protect such rights as freedom and privacy?

• Is the position designed so that people are likely to help with the exercise of its powers?

7. How could you change the position to correct any weaknesses you have identified?

8. Should the position be kept as it is, changed, or eliminated? Explain your decision about the position in terms of the strengths and weaknesses involved.

What do you think?

1. How might this set of intellectual tools be useful in evaluating positions of authority?

2. Why is it important to be able to evaluate positions of authority?

Using the Lesson

1. Select a position of authority that you have seen on television or read about in a newspaper, magazine, or book. Use the intellectual tools you have just learned in this lesson to evaluate the position.

2. Write a short story describing what might happen in a country where the position of president has not been planned well.

6. 该职位有什么优势和劣势？

　　• 是否经过精心设计以实现其目标？

　　• 是否有足够的权力——充分但不过度？

　　• 是否有办法使担任这一职位的人为自己的行为负责？

　　• 该职位是否负担过重？

　　• 是否有足够的资源来履行该职位的职责？

　　• 是否有适度的公共沟通和投入？

　　• 该职位是否必须在行使权力时使用公正和人道的程序？

　　• 设计该职位是否旨在保护例如自由和隐私这样的权利？

　　• 设计该职位是不是为了能帮助人们行使其权力？

7. 为纠正你们之前找出的设计缺陷，你们将如何改变该职位？

8. 应当让该职位保持现状？还是改变它？还是取消它？根据该职位所包含的优势和劣势，解释你们的决定。

你怎么看?

1. 这组知识工具如何能在评估权威职位时发挥作用？

2. 为什么能够评估权威职位是非常重要的？

知识运用

1. 当你看电视或阅读报纸、杂志和书籍时，留意并选择一个权威职位。运用你在这一课中所学到的知识工具来评估这个职位。

2. 写一个小故事，描述一个国家的总统职位若设计不当可能会发生的状况。

LESSON 11

How Would You Evaluate This Position of Authority?

Purpose of Lesson

In this lesson you role-play a naval review board hearing that has been convened to consider the authority of a ship's captain. You evaluate this position of authority using the intellectual tools you studied in the last lesson.

When you have completed the lesson, you should be able to explain and defend the position you have taken on the authority ofa ship's captain.

Terms to Know

flogging

Critical Thinking Exercise

EVALUATING A POSITION OF AUTHORITY

The following selection has been adapted from Richard Henry Dana's book, Two Years Before the Mast (1840). It tells of a young sailor's adventures at sea. The problem described by the sailor in "A Flogging at Sea" was probably not an isolated incident. Therefore, the Naval Review Board wanted to evaluate the authority held by ship's captains.

Your teacher will divide your class into groups and assign each group one of the following roles:

- Narrator
- Captain
- Sam, a sailor
- John, a sailor
- Naval Review Board

第十一课：如何评估一个权威职位？

本课目标

在这一课里，你们要角色扮演，召开一次海军审查委员会的模拟听证会，主要讨论船长的权威。运用在上一课中学到的知识工具来评估这个权威职位。

学完本课后，你们应当能够解释并论证自己有关船长权威的观点。

掌握词汇

鞭刑

重点思考练习

评估一个权威职位

以下阅读材料改编自理查德·亨利·达纳的《两年水手生涯》（1840）。它讲述了一个年轻水手的海上冒险经历。通过船员描述自己亲身经历的"海上鞭刑"很可能不是单个案例，因此，海军审查委员会希望能重新评估船长所拥有的权威。

老师将会把你们班分组，并指定各组分别扮演以下角色：

· 故事讲述者
· 船长
· 山姆，一名水手
· 约翰，一名水手
· 海军审查委员会

First, each group will read the "Background," the "Job Description," "A Flogging at Sea," and the "Postscript" and then complete the intellectual tool chart on p. 170. Next, the groups representing characters in the story will develop testimony to present to the Naval Review Board, and will select a spokesperson to present the group's testimony. All group members should be prepared to answer questions from the Naval Review Board, however. Meanwhile, the group playing the Naval Review Board will develop questions to ask each group and will select a chairperson to conduct the hearing. After all groups have presented their testimony, the Naval Review Board should discuss the scope and limits of the authority of a ship's captain, and decide whether to make any changes in the position, keep it as it is, or eliminate it. The Board should explain its decision to the class.

How much authority should a ships captain be given. ☞

首先,每组将依次阅读"背景材料"、"工作描述"、《海上的鞭刑》和"后记",然后完成第171页的知识工具表。其次,每组所扮演的人物将分别向海军审查委员会提交证据,并选出一名发言人代表陈述证词,但小组所有成员都应该准备回答海军审查委员会提出的问题。同时,扮演海军审查委员会的小组将列出询问各组的问题,并选出一名主席来主持听证会。在各组陈述完自己的证词后,海军审查委员会应当讨论如何界定一艘舰艇的船长权威的范围和限制,决定是否需要对该职位做出任何改变,还是维持现状,或者取消该职位。最后,委员会应当向全班解释自己的决定。

一艘船的船长应当被赋予多少权威?

The Background

The year is 1840. The Naval Review Board has decided to examine problems that occur on sailing ships and decide what should be done about them. Recently, a new problem has come to the board's attention because of a story written by a sailor. The story raises questions about the limits of authority of a ship's captain.

The Naval Review Board will conduct a hearing to evaluate the position of the ship's captain and gather suggestions for ways to improve the position. To help you do this, you will have the following:

• a ship's captain's job description

• the sailor's story, "A Flogging at Sea"

• an intellectual tool chart that will help you evaluate the position and make suggestions for improvement

 If you served on a Naval Review Board, what information would you need before suggesting changes in the authority of a ship's captain? ☞

背景材料

　　故事的背景是 1840 年，海军审查委员会决定要审查航行出海的船舶上出现的问题，并决定应当如何解决这些问题。最近，由于一部新出版的水手写的小说，委员会注意到了一个新问题。这部小说提出了一艘舰艇船长的权威的限制问题。

　　海军审查委员会将举行一次听证会，来评估该船长的职位，同时要收集关于改进这一职位的建议。为了帮助你们完成这一目标，你们应当掌握以下几份材料：

- 一份船长的"职位描述"
- 那位水手的故事：《海上的鞭刑》
- 一张知识工具表，它将有助于评估该职位，并提出改进建议

Ship's Captain: A Job Description

Duties and Powers. A ship's captain has the duty and the power to do the following:

- supervise the running of the ship
- decide the course of the ship
- assign people to different jobs on board ship
- settle disagreements among sailors
- punish sailors who break rules
- decide who will receive special privileges (such as shore leave)
- write reports to the ship's owners
- keep a daily log of the ship's progress
- represent the ship's owners whenever the ship reaches a foreign port

Privileges. A ship's captain is entitled to receive the following:

- a salary from the ship's owners and a percentage of the profits from the voyage
- a special uniform
- a private cabin
- specially prepared food

Limitations. A ship's captain may not do the following:

- risk the success of the voyage
- break the law of the land in a foreign port
- punish by death sailors who have broken rules

A Flogging at Sea

The captain of our ship had been losing his temper about a lot of little things. He threatened to flog the cook for throwing wood on deck. He became furious when the first mate bragged that he could tie knots better than the captain. He directed most of his anger to a large man called Sam. Sam could not speak very well and he was a little slow. Yet he was a pretty good sailor and tried his best. The captain just didn't like him.

One Saturday morning, I heard him shouting at someone. Then I heard noises that sounded like a fight.

船长：职位描述

职责和权力。一艘船舶的船长有责任和权力做以下事：

- 监督船舶的运行
- 决定船舶的航行路线
- 在船上分配船员做不同的工作
- 调解船员之间的纠纷
- 惩罚违反规定的船员
- 决定谁将会获得特别优待（例如离船岸权假期）
- 向船舶所有者撰写报告
- 写航海日记，报告船舶航行进度
- 到达国外港口时代表船舶所有者

特权。一艘船舶的船长被赋予获得以下：

- 从船舶所有者处领取薪水，并从航程中获得一定比例的利润
- 一身特殊制服
- 一间私人舱室
- 专门准备的食物

限制。一艘船舶的船长可能无法做以下事：

- 不顾航行安全的冒险行为
- 在国外港口触犯当地法律
- 对违反规定的船员处以死刑

《海上的鞭刑》

我们的船长对很多小事都忍不住发脾气。因为厨子把木材丢到甲板上，船长就威胁要鞭打他。大副吹嘘他打的结比船长更好，船长就非常生气。他常常把怒气发泄在大个子山姆身上。山姆不太会说话，动作也有点慢，但他是个不错的水手，并很努力工作，可船长就是不喜欢他。

一个星期六早上，我听到船长朝某人怒吼，然后，我听到像打架的声音。

"You may well keep still, for I have you," said the captain. 'Will you ever talk back to me again?"

"I never did, sir," said Sam.

"That's not what I asked you. Will you ever talk back to me again?"

"I never did, sir," Sam repeated.

"Answer my question or I'll make a spread eagle of you! I'll flog you!" The captain was almost beside himself with anger.

"I'm no slave," said Sam.

"Then I'll make you one," said the captain. He sprang to the deck and called to the first mate, 'Tie that man up! Make a spread eagle of him! I'll teach you all who is the master of this ship!" The mate took Sam to the deck. Sam did not struggle.

"What are you going to flog that man for, sir?" said John, a sailor to the captain. The captain turned and ordered other sailors to put him in irons.

By this time the first mate had tied Sam, taken off his jacket, and bared his back. The captain stood a few feet away so he could have a good swing at him. In his hand he held a thick, strong rope.

Watching this made me feel sick. I wanted to stop it, but there were only a few others who felt as I did. The captain and his officers outnumbered us. If we started a fight, we would lose. Then they would accuse us of mutiny. Even if we could win, they would brand us as pirates for life. If they ever caught us, they would severely punish us. A sailor has no rights. He has to do whatever the captain orders, or he becomes a mutineer or pirate.

Swinging as hard as he could, the captain lashed into poor Sam's back. Six times he struck Sam with the rope.

"Will you ever talk back to me again?" shouted the captain.

Sam said nothing. Three more times the captain flogged him. Finally he cut Sam down and sent him to the front of the ship.

"Now you," said the captain, walking to John and taking off the irons. The first mate tied John and the captain prepared to flog him.

"Why are you flogging me, sir?" asked John. "Have I ever refused my duty? Have I ever been lazy or talked back?"

"你最好给我站着别动，"船长说："你还敢再跟我顶嘴？"

"我从来没有，先生，"山姆说。

"那不是我问你的。你还敢不敢再跟我顶嘴？"

"我从来没有，先生，"山姆重复道。

"回答我的问题，不然我会把你绑成大字型！我会鞭打你！"船长几乎气到发疯。

"我不是奴隶，"山姆说。

"那我就让你当一回！"船长说。他跳上甲板叫大副："把那个人绑起来！让他好看！四肢展开！我要让你们看看谁才是这艘船的船长！"船员把山姆带到了甲板上，山姆并没有挣扎。

"你要鞭打这个人做什么，先生？"一名水手约翰说。船长转身就命令其他船员给约翰带上铁镣。

大副在把山姆绑起来的时候脱掉了他的上衣，露出他的背部。船长特意站在几英尺之外，这样可以好好用力鞭打他，手上还攥着一根又粗又重的绳子。

看着这一切使我感到很不舒服。我想制止，但没几个人跟我想的一样。船长和他的下属人数众多，如果开打，我们铁定会输，然后他们就会指控我们叛变。即使我们能获胜，他们也会给我们终生打上海盗的标签。一旦抓到我们，他们会加倍严厉地惩罚我们。一个水手没有权利，他必须做船长命令的所有事，要么他就变成一个叛徒或海盗。

船长用尽全身力气，甩着绳子鞭打着可怜的山姆，一共6鞭。

"你还敢不敢再顶嘴？"船长咆哮着。

山姆什么都没有说。船长又打了3鞭，然后他切断山姆身上的绳索，把他放在船舷最前面。

"现在轮到你，"船长说着，走到约翰身边，摘掉他的铁镣。大副把约翰绑起来，船长准备要鞭打他了。

"你为什么要鞭打我，先生？"约翰问。"难道我曾经拒绝尽责？难道我曾经偷懒或顶嘴？"

"No," answered the captain, "I'm flogging you because you ask questions."

"Aren't I allowed to ask questions?" asked John.

"No!" shouted the captain. "I will not allow anyone to do anything unless I tell them to." He started flogging John. He reached way back to hit harder and harder. The more he flogged, the wilder he became. I was horrified. I couldn't watch anymore. At last the captain stopped and the first mate cut John down. The captain turned to the rest of us.

"Now you see how things are! Now you know who I am! I'm the slave driver and you are my slaves! I'll make you all do as I say or I'll flog the lot of you!"

Postscript

Those who have followed me in my narrative will remember that I was witness to an act of great cruelty inflicted upon my own shipmates; and indeed the simple mention of the word flogging brings up in me feelings which I can hardly control. Yet, when the proposition is made to abolish it entirely and at once; to prohibit the captain from ever, under any circumstances, inflicting corporal punishment, I am obliged to pause.

I should not wish to take the command of a ship tomorrow and know, and have my crew know, that I could not, under any circumstances, inflict even moderate chastisement. I should trust that I might never have to resort to it; and, indeed, I scarcely know what risk I would not run, and to what inconvenience I would not subject myself, rather than do so. Yet not to have the power of holding it up as a threat and indeed of protecting myself, and all under my charge, by it, if some extreme case should arise, would be a situation I should not wish to be placed in myself, or to take the responsibility of placing another in.

"不，"船长说："我鞭打你因为你刚问问题了。"

"我不能提问吗？"约翰问。

"不能！"船长喊道："我不会允许任何人做任何事情，除非是我的命令！"他开始鞭打约翰。他打得越来越用力，越打越疯狂。我被吓坏了，再也看不下去了。最后，船长停下来，大副解开约翰的绳索把他放下来。船长转向我们其他人：

"现在你们看到了！现在你们知道我是谁了！我是奴隶主，你们都是我的奴隶！我会让你们听我的命令做事，不然就抽你们鞭子！"

后　记

那些听过我的讲述的人都会记得，我亲眼目睹了那件发生在我的伙伴身上非常残忍的事。事实上，单是提到"鞭刑"这个词都会让我不可遏制地想起当时的感受。然而，当有提案要求完全并立即废止"鞭刑"、从此禁止船长在任何情况下施以体罚的时候，我不得不要求暂停这一提案。

因为如果我是船长，我和我的船员都知道在任何情况下船长都不能实施哪怕是最轻微的惩罚，那么我应该就不会接管明天出海的那艘船。我相信自己可能永远不会使用暴力，但事实上，我自己也不知道我会拒绝承担怎样的风险，我也不能确定自己一定不会遇到麻烦，还不如就索性这么做（实施暴力）。然而，如果没有一种可以作为威胁的权力去阻止风险并切实保护我自己，如果没有一种我能掌控一切的权力，那么一旦出现某些极端状况，我既不愿意自己被带入那样的处境，也不愿意承担任何让别人也落入那种境地的责任。

Using the Lesson

1. Can you think of any circumstances that might require someone to have absolute authority? If so, what are they? Why do they require unchecked power to be used at the sole discretion of the person in authority?

2. As a class project, arrange to have a person in a position of authority (police officer, judge, district attorney, public defender, or mayor) visit your classroom. Ask that person to describe and evaluate the duties, powers, privileges, and limitations of the authority of his or her position.

知识运用

1. 试想想，在什么情况下会需要某个人拥有绝对的权威？如果有，应该是怎样的情况下？为什么需要让掌握权威职位的人行使这种没有制约的权力，一切都凭他或她自行决定？

2. 制定一个班级计划，安排一位担任权威职位的人（警察、法官、地区检察官、公设辩护人或市长）访问你们班，请他或她描述并评估自己所担任的权威职位的职责、权力、特权和限制。

Intellectual Tool Chart for Evaluating Positions of Authority	
Questions	**Answers**
1. What position of authority is to be evaluated?	
2. What is the purpose of the position?	
3. Is the position necessary? Why or why not?	
4. What are the duties, powers, privileges, and limitations of the position?	
5. What might be the consequences of this position as it is designed?	
6. What are the weaknesses (if any) in the way the position is designed? Consider: • number of duties • resources provided • grant and limitation of power • accountability • controls to prevent misuse of authority • requirement of fair procedures and respect for important values	
7. What changes would you suggest to improve the position? What would be the benefits and costs of these changes?	
8. Do you think the position should be eliminated, left as it is, or changed? Explain your reasoning.	

评估权威职位的知识工具表	
问题	答案
1. 要评估的权威职位是什么？	
2. 这个职位的目的是什么？	
3. 这个职位是必要的吗？为什么是？为什么不是？	
4. 这个职位的职责、权力、特权和限制是什么？	
5. 这个职位在设计之初的结果可能是什么？	
6. 设计这个职位的方式有哪些劣势（如果有）？请考虑： ·职责的数目 ·提供的资源 ·授权和限制 ·问责制 ·防止权威被滥用的控制 ·公平程序的需要和对重要价值观的尊重	
7. 如果要改进该职位，你有什么建议？这些改进的利弊得失是什么？	
8. 你认为该职位应当被取消还是应当维持现状或被改变？解释你的推论。	

LESSON 12

What Should Be the Scope and Limits of Authority During Wartime?

Purpose of Lesson

In this lesson you consider two examples of the use of authority during wartime. The first concerns President Lincoln's exercise of authority at the beginning of the Civil War. The second concerns the government's treatment of Japanese Americans during World War II .You then participate in a debate on the issue of what the limits of authority should be during wartime.

When you have completed the lesson, you should be able to explain and defend the positions you have taken on the use of authority during wartime.

Terms to Know

dilemma	espionage
secede	internment camp
proclamation	writ of habeas corpus
blockade	sabotage

Critical Thinking Exercise

EXAMINING THE SCOPE AND LIMITS OF AUTHORITY DURING WARTIME

As you read these selections, think about the following question: Under what circumstances, if any, should a person in authority go beyond the normal limits of his or her authority? Work in small groups to answer the "What do you think?" questions that follow each selection.

第十二课：战争时期权威的范围和限制应当是什么？

本课目标

在这一课中，请思考两个战争时期行使权威的案例。第一个是林肯总统在南北战争初期的权威运用；第二个是第二次世界大战期间政府对日裔美国人的政策。然后你们将组织一次关于战争时期对权威应有什么限制的辩论。

完成本课学习后，你们应该能够解释和论证自己有关战争时期行使权威问题的观点。

掌握词汇

困境	间谍
脱离	蓄意破坏
公告	集中营
封锁	人身保护令

重点思考练习

研究战时权威的范围和限制

当你们阅读以下材料时，请思考：在什么情况下（如果有），担任权威职位的人应该超越他或她的权威的正常范围？分组回答每段阅读材料后面"你怎么看？"部分的问题。

Lincoln's Dilemma

Abraham Lincoln stood alone in his White House office one April night in 1861. He was facing a terrible dilemma. Hostility between the northern and southern states had been increasing, especially over the issue of slavery. Seven southern states had officially withdrawn from the United States. Southern troops had occupied federal forts and navy yards in those states. War seemed inevitable.

Then it happened. On April 12, 1861, Confederate troops fired on Fort Sumter at Charleston, South Carolina. Northern troops returned the fire. The Civil War had begun. Lincoln hoped that he could end the war in a short time and save the Union. He knew that to end the war quickly, he would have to act fast and perhaps take some actions unauthorized by the Constitution.

This was Lincoln's dilemma: He had sworn "an oath registered in Heaven" to uphold and defend the Constitution. He also had promised his fellow citizens to save the Union. He believed that without the Union, the Constitution would be little more than a scrap of paper. He believed that this threat to the nation's existence called for the exercise of the government's powers of self-preservation.

On April 15, 1861, Lincoln issued a proclamation calling 75,000 members of the state militias to fight the Southern rebellion. In that same proclamation, Lincoln called for Congress to convene on July 4, almost three months later. Lincoln was determined to bring an end to the war without interference from Congress or anyone else.

On April 19, Lincoln ordered a blockade on the seaports of all seceded states.

On April 20, he ordered an additional nineteen vessels for the naval fleets. He extended the blockade to the ports of North Carolina and Virginia.

What might be the proper limits to presidential authority during wartime? ☞

林肯的困境

1861 年 4 月的一个晚上，亚伯拉罕·林肯独自站在他的白宫办公室里。此时的他面临着一个可怕的困境。南北方各州之间的敌意不断加剧，特别是在奴隶制问题上。南方 7 个州已正式宣布退出美利坚合众国，南方军队已经占领了这些州的联邦要塞和海军船坞，战争看起来是不可避免的了。

战争终究还是爆发了。1861 年 4 月 12 日，在南卡罗来纳州查尔斯顿，南方邦联军队对萨姆特堡开火，北方部队进行了回击，南北战争开始了。林肯希望他能在很短的时间内结束战争，拯救联邦。他知道，为了让战争快点结束，他不得不迅速采取行动，甚至一些宪法没有授权他的行动。

这正是林肯面对的两难局面：他曾"向上帝庄严宣誓"，要维护和捍卫合众国宪法，他也向他的同胞们保证过要保卫联邦。他相信，如果联邦不复存在了，宪法将只不过是一纸空文。他认为，这将是对国家生存的威胁，政府有权力进行自我保护。

1861 年 4 月 15 日，林肯发表了一份公告，征召 75000 名各州民兵与南方叛军作战，在公告里林肯还宣布在三个月后的 7 月 4 日召开国会。林肯决心要在不受国会或任何人的干涉下结束这场战争。

4 月 19 日，林肯下令封锁所有脱离联邦的南方各州的港口。

4 月 20 日，他下令再增派 19 艘海军战舰组成的舰队，将封锁范围扩大到北卡罗来纳州和弗吉尼亚州的港口。

什么是对战争时期总统权威的适当限制？

On May 3, he issued a nationwide call for 42,000 volunteers and enlarged the regular army by 24,000 and the navy by 18,000. This proclamation was contrary to Article I of the Constitution that gives Congress the power to "raise and support armies" and "to provide and maintain a navy."

On April 20, he directed the Secretary of the Treasury to pay $2 million to three private individuals in New York to provide supplies for the military, even though the Constitution provides, "no money shall be drawn from the Treasury but in consequence of appropriations made by law." Lincoln said that this move was necessary because there were so many disloyal persons in the government.

Lincoln also took steps to maintain public order in the North and to prevent interference with the war effort. He authorized the suspension of the writ of habeas corpus in certain areas; this meant that people could be arrested and held without any opportunity to go before a judge. He forbade the post office to process "treasonable correspondence." When Congress met on July 4, Lincoln greeted them with a special message asking for approval of his actions. In his paper he argued that every constitutional government must have the power of self-preservation and that in the American government the president exercised this power. In this message, he wrote about his actions since April 12: These measures, whether strictly legal or not, were ventured upon under what appeared to be a popular demand and a public necessity....

What do you think?

1. How did President Lincoln's exercise of authority exceed the scope and limits of the constitutional authority of his position?

2. What arguments can you make to justify President Lincoln's actions? What values and interests underlie these arguments?

3. What arguments can you make to oppose President Lincoln's actions? What values and interests underlie these arguments?

4. Why might it be important to limit the authority of government officials? If we allow exceptions to these limits, why might it be important to clearly define the circumstances under which we permit the exceptions?

5月3日，他向全国发出呼吁，征召42000名志愿军人，将正规军扩大到24000人，海军增扩到18000人。这项公告违背了宪法第一条中赋予国会（而不是总统）的有关"募集和维持陆军"和"配备和保持海军"的权力。

4月20日，林肯委派财政部长支付200万美元给纽约的3个私营企业主，以便为军队提供军事物资补给。然而宪法规定："除了依照法律的规定拨款之外，不得自国库中提出任何款项。"林肯认为此举是必要的，因为有太多不忠于政府的人。

林肯也采取各项措施以维持北方社会的公共秩序，并防止对战争努力的一切干扰。他授权在某些地区暂缓执行人身保护令：这意味着任何人都可以被逮捕并且没有任何机会接受审判。他也禁止邮局办理"叛国性质的信函"。

7月4日国会召开，林肯在致国会议员的信中，要求国会批准他的一切行动。他指出每个宪政政府必须有自我保护的权力，在美国政府中应当由总统行使这项权力。他是这样描述自己从4月12日以来的行动的："这些措施，无论严格意义上是否合法，都似乎是一种普遍要求与公开需要之下的冒险。"

你怎么看？

1. 林肯总统行使权威是如何超出了宪法赋予总统这一权威职位的范围和限制？

2. 有什么论据可以证明林肯总统的行动是正当的？这些论据当中包含了什么价值观和利益？

3. 有什么论据可以用来反对总统林肯的行动？这些论据当中包含了什么价值观和利益？

4. 为什么必须限制政府官员的权威？如果我们允许这些限制当中存在例外，为什么必须明确界定被允许的例外的具体情况？

The Internment of Japanese Americans

Following the Japanese attack on Pearl Harbor m December 1941, the United States entered World War II by declaring war against Japan, Germany, and Italy. Never in the history of the nation had the American people faced such a difficult military challenge. The United States had to fight major wars in two faraway parts of the globe: Europe and the Far East. Conducting a war on two fronts simultaneously was extremely difficult, but most Americans believed that they were fighting for their country's freedom and security. They believed that the future of the nation was in their hands.

At the time of the Pearl Harbor attack, more than 125,000 Japanese Americans lived in the United States, mostly on the West Coast. More than two-thirds of these people were United States citizens. Although there never had been a case of espionage or sabotage by an American of Japanese descent, many people feared that it could happen. Japanese Americans had long suffered from racial discrimination and prejudice in the United States.

The situation worsened with the attack on Pearl Harbor. Shocked by the early Japanese victories in the South Pacific, many Americans feared that the Japanese might invade the West Coast.

On February 19, 1942, President Roosevelt responded to this fear by issuing an executive order. This order allowed American military commanders to relocate people of Japanese ancestry from the West Coast to camps further inland. The relocation program made no distinction between citizens and aliens.

 What were the consequences when the government used its authority to relocate citizens of Japanese ancestry to internment camps during World War II? ☞

日裔美国人集中营

1941 年 12 月日本偷袭珍珠港事件后，美国对日本、德国和意大利宣战，正式参加第二次世界大战。在本国历史上美国人民从来没有面临过这样一个棘手的军事挑战。美国必须在地球上相距遥远的两个战场分头作战：欧洲和远东地区。虽然在两条战线上作战是极其艰难的，但大多数美国人认为，他们是为了国家的自由和安全而战。他们相信，国家的未来在他们手中。

在日本偷袭珍珠港事件发生时，有超过 12.5 万日裔美国人生活在美国，主要集中在西海岸。这些人当中超过三分之二是美国公民。虽然从来没有发生过日裔美国人卷入间谍案或阴谋破坏案件的情况，但许多人还是担心会发生类似事情。在美国，日裔美国人长期遭受种族歧视和偏见，随着珍珠港事件的爆发，这种情况更加恶化。战争初期日本在南太平洋战场的胜利使许多美国人担心日本可能会入侵美国西岸。

1942 年 2 月 19 日，罗斯福总统颁布了一项行政命令，以应对国民的这种恐惧。该命令允许美国军事指挥官将西岸的日裔居民"重新安置"到更远的内陆地区。这一迁移方案并没有区别日裔居民中的美国公民和外国人。

二战时期，政府运用其权威将日裔美国公民迁往集中营产生了什么结果？

The presidential executive order also gave military commanders the authority to declare certain places "military areas." The military commander could, at his discretion, exclude anyone from these military areas to prevent spying or sabotage. On March 2, 1942, Congress passed a law stating that anyone in a military area who disobeyed the orders of the military commander of that area could be sent to prison, fined, or both.

On May 3, 1942, General De Witt, the commander of the San Leandro, California, military area, issued Civilian Exclusion Order No. 34. This order stated that after May 9, 1942, all persons of Japanese ancestry would be excluded from San Leandro. The order said that the reason for this exclusion was the possibility of the "presence of. ... disloyal [to the United States members of the group." Before the end of 1942, the entire West Coast had been declared a "military area," and persons of Japanese descent had been ordered to internment camps by similar exclusion orders.

During the war, the military forcibly moved approximately 120,000 Japanese Americans from their homes to internment camps further inland. No charges were filed against these individuals; no claim of actual espionage or sabotage, or of any other crime, was asserted to justify their relocation and internment. Most were required to remain in the internment camps for the duration of the war-essentially imprisoned for three years. Businesses had to be abandoned; homes and other property were similarly lost.

　　此项总统行政命令也给予军事指挥官一定的权威，允许他们宣布某些地域为"军事区"，军事指挥官可以自行决定将任何人驱逐出自己的军事区，以防止间谍或破坏活动。1942 年 3 月 2 日，国会通过了一项法律规定：一旦军事区内任何人违背了该地区军事指挥官的命令，都将被送进监狱，或被罚款，或两者兼而有之。

　　1942 年 5 月 3 日，加利福尼亚州圣莱安德罗军事区的指挥官德威特将军发布了第 34 号驱逐平民令。命令要求：从 1942 年 5 月 9 日开始，所有日裔居民都将被驱逐出圣莱安德罗军事区。该命令指出，此次驱逐的原因是："存在对（美国）团体成员不忠"的可能性。1942 年年底前，整个西海岸已被宣布为"军事区"，日裔居民都被类似命令要求前往集中营。

　　在战争期间，军队强行迁移了大约 12 万日裔美国人离开家园，前往遥远的内陆，住进集中营。这些人并没有受到任何指控，没有进行任何实质的间谍或阴谋破坏活动，或犯有任何罪行，没有任何证据能证明强迫他们迁移到集中营的行为是正当的。大部分日裔美国人都被要求待在集中营里直到战争结束——实际是被监禁了三年。他们不得不放弃自己的事业，也失去了家园和财产。

What do you think?

1. What were some consequences of the following three exercises of authority? Which consequences were benefits, and which were costs?

- President Roosevelt's Executive Order of February 19, 1942

- The law passed by Congress on March 2, 1942

- Civilian Exclusion Order No. 34 issued by General De Witt on May 9, 1942

2. What might have been the consequences if President Roosevelt had lacked the authority to issue the Executive Order of February 19, 1942? If Congress had lacked the authority to pass the March 2, 1942 law? If General De Witt had lacked the authority to issue Civilian Exclusion Order No. 34?

3. Do you think the internment of Japanese Americans during World War II illustrates the need to relax constitutional limitations during wartime, or the need to maintain constitutional limitations even when the country is at war? Explain your position.

Preparing for aClass Debate

Now that you have considered the selections on pp. 174-180, your class will debate the following issue:

RESOLVED: That the president should be allowed to exceed the constitutional limits on his or her authority during wartime.

To prepare for the debate, your class will be divided into four groups, two on each side of the issue. One group on each side will present initial arguments supporting or opposing the resolution. The other group on each side will present rebuttal arguments, responding to and challenging the initial arguments the group anticipates the other side will make. Each group will have five minutes to make its presentation, and should select two or three spokespersons to present the group's arguments. The remainder of each group, after participating in the preparation of the group's presentation, will form the audience for the debate.

你怎么看?

1. 下列三种权威的运用产生了哪些结果? 其中哪些结果是利益(好处),
   哪些是弊病(损失)?

   1942 年 2 月 19 日罗斯福总统的行政令;

   1942 年 3 月 2 日国会通过的法律;

   1942 年 5 月 9 日将军德威特签发的第 34 号驱逐平民令。

2. 如果罗斯福总统没有权威签发 1942 年 2 月 29 日的行政令,可能会产
   生什么结果? 如果国会没有权威通过 1942 年 3 月 2 日的法律,可能
   会有什么结果? 如果将军德威特没有权威签发第 34 号平民驱逐令,
   又可能会有什么结果?

3. 你认为第二次世界大战期间日裔美国人集中营是否说明了战争时期有
   放松宪法限制的需要? 或者即便是当国家处于战争时期必须保持宪
   法的限制? 请解释你的观点。

准备一场全班辩论

现在请思考第 175 — 181 页的阅读材料,你们班将准备就以下问题
进行辩论:

决议:应该允许总统在战争时期超越宪法对他或她的权威限制。

为了准备辩论,你们班将被分为四组,每方各有两组。每一方其中一
组提出支持或反对该决议的初始论据;另一组代表将反驳论据,回应并挑
战你们组估计辩论对手会提出的初始论据。每个小组将有 5 分钟做陈述发
言,并应选出两个或三个发言人陈述本组论据。其他组员在参与各准备阶
段的工作之后,在辩论阶段转做观众。

Conducting the Debate

One student from the audience should be selected to serve as the moderator of the debate, and another should serve as timekeeper. The moderator will briefly introduce the topic, and state the resolution to be debated. The group presenting initial arguments in favor of the resolution will make their presentation first, followed by the group presenting initial arguments against the resolution. The order is reversed for rebuttal arguments, with the group presenting arguments against the resolution going first, followed by the group presenting arguments in favor of the resolution. At the conclusion of the debate, the audience may vote on the resolution. The class as a whole should discuss how the debate affected their views on the issue, which arguments were persuasive, which were not, and why.

Using the Lesson

1. Issues regarding the internment of Japanese Americans during World War II reached the United States Supreme Court in the cases of Hirabayashi v. United States, 320 U.S. 81 (1943), Korematsu v. United States, 323 U.S. 214 (1944), and Exparte Endo, 323 U.S. 283 (1944). Find out what happened in these cases, and report what you learn to the class. In your report, be sure to explain your views about how the Supreme Court dealt with the cases.

2. What might be the dangers of allowing limitations on authority to be superseded in emergencies? Before World War II, the Geffilan Constitution contained "emergency" provisions (Articles 25 and 48) which were instrumental in Hitler's assumption of dictatorial powers. Do research to find out what these emergency provisions authorized, what safeguards and limitations existed to prevent abuse of these emergency provisions, and evaluate why these safeguards and limitations proved ineffective.

3. Work with several classmates to prepare a simulated television interview with a Japanese American citizen who the government forced to live in an internment camp. In preparation for the interview, you may do additional research on the camps. Your teacher can suggest books for you to read.

进行辩论

应从观众中选出一位同学担任辩论的主持，另外选出一位做计时员。主持人将简要介绍并说明辩论的题目和决议。正方中负责陈述初始论据的第一组应当首先进行陈述，紧接着是反方陈述初始论据的小组发言。在反驳论据的阶段，发言顺序与之前相反，反方代表首先陈述论据，紧跟着是正方。在辩论结束时，观众必须对决议进行投票。全班应当一起讨论这次辩论如何影响了自己对问题的看法，哪些论据是有说服力的，哪些没有，并解释原因。

知识运用

1. 第二次世界大战期间日裔美国人集中营的问题最终提交到了美国联邦最高法院，分别为"1943 年平林诉美利坚合众国案，320U.S.81"，"1944 年惟松诉美利坚合众国案，323U.S.214"以及"1944 年远藤诉美利坚合众国案，323U.S.283"。查阅这些诉讼案的经过，并将你的发现向全班报告。要在你的报告中解释自己对上述诉讼案中最高法院的裁决的看法。

2. 在紧急情况下允许取消权威的限制，可能会导致什么危险？第二次世界大战之前，德国宪法中包含的"紧急状态"条文（第 25 条和第 48 条），变成了希特勒获得独裁权力的工具。研究调查这些应急规定授权的内容，查找以前存在过哪些保障措施和限制来防止这些应急规定被滥用，并评估这些保障措施和限制被证明无效的原因。

3. 与几个同学一起准备一次模拟电视采访，采访一位被政府强迫住进集中营的日裔美国公民。在准备采访的过程中，你可以对集中营做更多的研究，你的老师可以为你推荐参考阅读书籍。

LESSON 13
How Would You Design a Position of Authority?

Purpose of Lesson

In this lesson you use the knowledge and skills you have acquired to decide the scope and limits of authority of a particular position. When you have completed this lesson you should be able to design the duties, powers, privileges, and limitations of a position of authority.

Terms to Know

hypothetical

Critical Thinking Exercise
DESIGNING APOSITION OF AUTHORITY

Your class will be dealing with a problem in a hypothetical school known as Taft High. Read the story below and divide into small groups of about three to five students. Each group will act as one of the student government committees assigned to develop a new position of authority at Taft High. Members of each group should read the "Directions for the Committees" and answer the questions. After each group has made its presentation, the class should discuss what would be the best solution to the problem at Taft High.

第十三课：如何设计一个权威职位?

本课目标

在这一课里，你们将运用之前学到的知识和技能来判断某个特定权威职位的范围和限制。学完本课后，你们应当能够设计出一个权威职位的职责、权力、特权和限制。

掌握词汇

假设

重点思考练习

设计一个权威职位

假设在塔夫脱高等中学中存在着一些问题，而你们班需要解决这些问题。阅读下面的故事，将全班分组，每组 3 至 5 人。每一组都将扮演塔夫脱高中的学生会，被指派要为塔夫脱高中设立一个新的权威职位。每组成员都应当阅读"委员会指南"并回答当中的问题。小组陈述发言结束后，全班应当一起讨论什么是解决塔夫脱高中存在的问题的最好方法。

A Problem at Taft High School

There had been a student government at Taft High School for several years. Each semester students elected a student body president and representatives from each homeroom. The student government had the right to make some school rules and to plan special events such as sports activities and dances. Most of the students, teachers, and school administrators thought the student government did a good job.

During the past two years, trouble had been developing at the school. More students were breaking school rules, the number of fights had increased, and a feeling of tension replaced the previous easy-going atmosphere. In some cases, the principal accused students of breaking into lockers and stealing. There were rumors of certain students carrying weapons. The student restrooms were becoming dangerous places.

For many years, teachers and administrators had the responsibility of dealing with students accused of breaking rules. The law required them to take this responsibility. The increase in fighting and rule-breaking was creating a difficult situation for teachers. Many believed that they were spending more time disciplining students than teaching them. They thought that this was unfair to the students who wanted to learn.

How teachers dealt with discipline problems sometimes upset students. They believed that some teachers did not give a fair hearing to those accused of breaking rules. Most students agreed that teachers were too busy to take the time necessary to hear all sides of a dispute.

How would you design a position of authority to deal with violence and rule–breaking at school? ☞

塔夫脱高中的问题

塔夫脱高中有一个存在数年的学生会。每学期学生们会选出一个学生会主席和各班代表。学生会有权制定某些学校规章，也有权筹办某些特别活动，例如运动会和舞蹈表演等。大多数学生、老师和学校领导都认为学生会的工作做得很不错。

在过去的两年中，学校开始出现一些问题。越来越多的学生破坏校规，打架斗殴现象屡见不鲜，学校里往日温和轻松的气氛被紧张不安的情绪取代。校长时常接到指控，有学生撬开储物柜门盗窃财物。学校里也流传着谣言，说某些学生携带武器进校，学生休息室正逐步成为危险地方。

多年来，教师和行政人员都有责任处理学生违规问题，法律要求他们承担这项责任，打架斗殴和违规事件的日益增加也让老师们陷入困境。许多人认为，老师花费了更多的时间来管束学生的行为，而不是给学生上课，这对想要学习的学生来说很不公平。

此外，老师们处理违纪问题的方式有时也会让学生们很不满意。他们认为，某些老师并没有给被指控违规的学生举行一次公平的听证会。大多数学生认为，老师们太忙以至于没有时间听取争端各方的意见。

你要如何设计一个权威职位来解决学校的暴力和违规问题？

Many students believed that something should be done to improve the situation. At a student government meeting they discussed the problem of how to give suspected rule-breakers a fair hearing. Members of the student government, a number of teachers, and members of the school administration also attended the meeting. After a long discussion of the problems facing the school, the principal, Ms. Willis, spoke.

"We have a pretty good idea of the problem facing us," she said. "I want to turn its solution over to you, the student government. If your recommendations are reasonable, I'll go with them. Remember that under state law must maintain order at this school. So whatever you decide must agree with the law."

Everyone agreed that Ms. Willis's suggestion was fair. After the administrators and teachers left, one student suggested they needed a position of authority. The others agreed, and the student representatives broke into committees to work on the task of designing a position of authority for Taft High.

 What might be the proper scope and limits of a position of authority to deal with violence and rule breaking at school? ☞

　　许多学生认为应该做点什么来改善目前学校的状况。在学生会会议上，他们讨论了如何给涉嫌违规的学生以公平申诉的问题。学生会的成员、许多老师和部分学校管理人员出席了会议。在对学校目前面临的问题进行了长时间的讨论后，学校校长威利斯女士发言说道：

　　"对目前摆在我们面前的问题，现在有个很不错的主意，"她说："我想将把解决方案的决定权交给你们——学生会。如果你们的建议是合理的，我会支持。请记住，根据法律，我必须维持这所学校的秩序。所以，无论你们的决定是什么，都必须是合法的。"

　　大家一致认为威利斯女士的建议是公平的。学校行政管理人员老师们离开后，一名学生提议：学生会需要设立一个权威职位。其他人纷纷表示同意。学生代表立刻组织了委员会，担负起为塔夫脱高中设计一个权威职位的任务。

在学校里，负责处理暴力和违规问题的权威职位的适当范围和限制是什么？

Directions for the Committees

Each group should act as one of the student government committees assigned the job of developing a new position of authority at Taft High School. Select a chairperson to lead your discussion and a recorder to take notes. Use the chart on p. 194 to assist you in designing a position of authority. Read, discuss, and answer each question in the chart carefully.

When you have completed the chart, prepare a description of a new position at Taft High. Have the chairperson of your committee present your plan to the rest of the class. The presentation should include the following:

- a statement of the purpose of the position

- a description of the position listing its duties, powers, privileges, and limitations

- a statement of the probable consequences (costs and benefits) of creating the position. The class should discuss the strengths and weaknesses of each proposed position and attempt to reach a consensus on the design of a new position of authority for Taft High.

Using the Lesson

1. Did you agree with your class decision on designing a position of authority for Taft High? Write a letter to the editor of the Taft High newspaper either supporting or opposing the new position for the school.

2. Think about a problem in your neighborhood or town that creating a position of authority might help. Use what you have learned in this unit to design a position of authority to help solve this problem.

委员会指南

　　每个小组应代表一个学生委员会，目标是为塔夫脱高中设计一个权威职位。每组应选出一位主席引导各组讨论，并用录音机记录下来。第195页的表格将有助于你们设计权威职位。认真阅读、讨论并回答表格中的每个问题。

　　当你们完成该表格后，就应当开始着手准备如何描述你们为塔夫脱高中设计的新职位。请各小组主席代表各组向全班其他同学阐述自己小组的计划。陈述中应当包含以下内容：

- 说明职位目标
- 职位描述：列出该职位的职责、权力、特权和限制
- 描述设立该职位可能产生的结果（利弊得失）
- 全班应当讨论每个备选职位的优势和劣势，并试图对塔夫脱高中的新权威职位设计达成一项共识

知识运用

1. 你是否赞同你们班为塔夫脱高中设计的权威职位？写封信给塔夫脱高中报社的编辑，或支持或反对这一新设计的权威职位。

2. 想想你的邻居或你居住的城镇中有没有什么可以通过设立权威职位来解决的问题。运用在本单元中学到的知识，设计一个权威职位以帮助解决这个问题。

Intellectual Tool Chart for Designing Positions of Authority	
Questions	**Answers**
1. What problem or problems are you trying to solve?	
2. Would establishing a position of authority help, or are there better ways to deal with the problem?Explain your views.	
3. What type of position of authority is your group suggesting: • one position or more than one? • individual or committee? • elected or appointed? Explain the reasons for your choices.	
4. What duties, powers, privileges, and limitations should the position of authority have? Consider: • number of duties • resources provided • grant and limitation of power • accountability • controls to prevent misuse of authority • requirement of fair procedures and respectf or important values	
5. What would be the consequences of having such a position of authority? Consider the benefts and costs of the position as you have designed it.	

设计权威职位的知识工具	
问题	答案
1.你试图解决什么问题（一个或多个）？	
2. 设立一个权威职位是否有助于解决这个或这些问题？是否有更好的方式解决问题？	
3.你们组建议设立哪一种权威职位？ ·一个或超过一个职位？ ·个人或委员会？ ·选举或任命？ 解释你们的选择	
4. 这个权威职位应该有什么责任、权力、特权和限制？请考虑： ·职责的数目 ·提供的资源 ·授权和限制 ·问责制 ·防止权威被滥用的控制 ·对公平程序的需要和对重要价值观的尊重	
5. 担任这样一个权威职位会有什么结果？考虑你们设计的这个职位的利弊得失。	

LESSON 14
What Should Be the Limits on Challenging Authority?

Purpose of Lesson

This final lesson on authority provides an opportunity to evaluate the limits on challenging authority. You examine an act of civil disobedience adapted from the ancient Greek tragedy Antigone, written by Sophocles. The class debates the propriety of disobeying a law in order to follow the dictates of one's conscience.

When you have completed the lesson, you should be able to evaluate, take, and defend positions on what the limits should be on challenging authority.

Terms to Know

civil disobedience

higher law

What is the American tradition of civil disobedience?

In Unit Five you learned how to determine the scope and limits of a position of authority. You have seen what can happen when a position of authority is designed badly or when a person holding such a position misuses or abuses authority. The framers of our Constitution understood the importance of limiting authority. That is why they created the system of shared powers and checks and balances in our Constitution. They designed the Bill of Rights to further protect individual liberties against possible abuse by those in authority.

Our constitutional system of government is based on majority rule, but it also protects individual rights and the rights of minorities. It allows those who do not agree with the decisions of the government to protest those decisions band try to change them. The following are some of the ways people can express their opinions:

第十四课：对挑战权威应当有怎样的限制？

本课目标

本课是关于权威的最后一课。在这一课中，你们将有机会评估挑战权威的限度。你们会读到一部关于公民的不服从权利的话剧，改编自索福克勒斯撰写的古希腊悲剧《安提戈涅》。然后全班要对不服从法律以遵循个人良知的正当性问题进行辩论。

学完本课后，你们应该能够评估、陈述和论证有关挑战权威应有的限制问题方面自己的观点。

掌握词汇

公民的不服从
更高的法律

美国公民不服从的传统是什么？

在第五单元中，你们已经学过如何确定权威职位的范围和限制，你们也了解某个设计不当的权威职位所产生的结果，也知道如果担任权威职位的人误用、滥用权威会发生什么事。正是由于美国宪法的制定者们认识到了限制权威的重要性，因此他们在我们的宪法中设立了权力分持和权力制衡制度。同时，他们也提出了《人权法案》，以进一步保护个人自由免于被当权者滥用的可能。

美国的宪政制度是基于多数人统治的，但它也保护个人权利和少数人的权利。它允许那些不同意政府决策的人反抗决策并试图改变决策。以下是某些人们可以表达个人观点的途径：

- voting
- writing letters to the media or to a public official
- signing petitions
- joining a protest group or political organization
- marching in demonstrations
- participating in boycotts

What happens when such forms of protest are not enough? What if you believe that it is against your moral or religious principles to support a law and all your legal efforts to change that law have failed? What choices do you have? How far should a person go in challenging authority?

These are very difficult questions. For centuries philosophers and scholars have been trying to find the answers. Throughout history, people have refused to obey laws they believed were unjust or morally wrong and have chosen to suffer the consequences of their actions, no matter how severe. Some people have chosen to engage in rebellion or revolution; others have looked to less violent forms of protest.

 Which forms of protest are acceptable, and which forms of protest are not? ☞

- 投票
- 向媒体或向公职人员写信
- 签署请愿书
- 参加抗议团体或政治组织
- 参加示威游行
- 参与杯葛

　　如果缺乏某些上述抗议形式时，会发生什么事？如果你认为支持某项法律违背了你的道德或宗教原则，同时你试图改变该项法律的所有合法努力都失败的情况下，又会发生什么事？个人挑战权威的范围有多大？

　　这些都是非常难以回答的问题。数百年来，哲学家和学者们都一直试图寻找问题的答案。纵观历史，人们曾经拒绝服从他们认为是不正义或道义上是错误的法律，也选择了承担自己的行为所带来的后果，无论那有多么严重。有些人选择参与叛乱或革命，还有人寻求不那么暴力的抗议形式。

哪种形式的抗议是可以接受的？哪种不是？

Civil disobedience is a form of nonviolent protest. It is an act done in defiance of a law or policy of the government to bring about change. Civil disobedience involves a willingness to accept the consequences involved. When we talk about civil disobedience, we are not simply talking about breaking the law. We are talking about a deliberate protest of a law or policy believed to be unjust. Such protest can take many forms. It may be a decision to do the following:

• not pay taxes

• burn a draft card

• help fugitive slaves

• chain oneself to a nuclear power plant

Civil disobedience is deeply rooted in the history of the United States and has, in some instances, led to profound changes in the Constitution. The abolitionists refused to recognize laws that supported slavery and preferred jail to a system they believed was immoral. They preferred to follow the "higher law" of their own religious and moral principles rather than the authority of the government.

Leaders of the woman suffrage, civil rights, and antiwar movements also chose to disobey laws and go to jail rather than support laws they believed were wrong. Rev. Martin Luther King, Jr., who was greatly influenced by the teachings of Mohandas Gandhi, wrote in his Letter from Birmingham City Jail, "I submit that an individual who breaks a law that his conscience tells him is unjust, and willingly accepts the penalty by staying in jail to arouse the conscience of the community over its injustice, is in reality expressing the very highest respect for the law."

 What questions did Mohandas Gandhi have to consider in choosing to use civil disobedience to challenge the authority of India's government during the 1940s? ☞

公民的不服从是一种非暴力的抗议形式，它是通过挑战一项法律或政府的政策而带来某些变化的行为。公民的不服从权利中也包括愿意承担自己的行为结果。因此当我们谈到公民的不服从权利时，我们并不仅是简单地谈论有关违反法律的话题。我们谈论的是有意识地反抗我们认为是不公平的法律或政策，这些反抗可以采用多种形式，其中可能包括：

· 不交税

· 烧毁征兵卡

· 帮助奴隶逃亡

· 把自己与一个核电厂绑在一起

公民的不服从权利深深植根于美国历史当中，并在某些情况下导致了宪法发生某些深刻的变化。废奴主义者拒绝承认支持奴隶制度的法律，宁愿坐牢也不愿接受他们认为是不道德的法律。他们更愿意遵从他们自己的宗教和道德原则这样"更高的法律"，而不是政府的权威。

妇女选举权、民权运动和反战运动的领袖也选择了不服从法律，宁愿坐牢也不愿支持自己认为是错误的法律。牧师小马丁·路德·金深受圣雄甘地的教诲影响，在他从伯明翰市监狱寄出的信中我们读到："我认为一个人打破了法律，他的良心告诉他法律是不正义的，并自觉接受留在监狱中的惩罚，希望引起社会良心对不正义的感知，这一举动实际上是表达了对法律非常崇高的敬意。"

20世纪40年代，圣雄甘地在选择用公民不服从权利挑战印度政府权威的时候应当考虑什么问题？

Civil disobedience is an extreme choice made only when there seems to be no other alternative. When is it an appropriate choice? In this lesson you will consider the limits on challenging authority. You may never engage in an act of civil disobedience, but you may very well confront laws that you believe are against your moral or religious principles. The following activity will help you think about some questions you should consider in such a situation. It will give you some tools to deal with a very difficult subject.

Critical Thinking Exercise

TAKING A POSITION ON THE CIVIL DISOBEDIENCE IN ANTIGONE

Read the story below, then follow the instructions for a class debate. The story is adapted from the Greek tragedy Antigone, written by Sophocles in 442 B.C. It tells of a young woman, Antigone, who violates a law to follow the dictates of her conscience and suffers the consequences.

The Tragedy of Antigone

When Antigone was about eighteen years old, her uncle Creon became ruler of Thebes, an important city in ancient Greece. Both Antigone and Creon were strong-willed; both believed deeply in what they thought was right. Because neither would give into the other, they brought great tragedy on both themselves and their city.

When is it right to disobey political authority? Antigone answered that question to her own satisfaction and died for it. Creon had a different answer and lost everything he loved.

Creon's Decree

Before Creon became king of Thebes, his brother Oedipus ruled the land. The former king had two daughters, Antigone and Ismene, and two sons, Eteocles and Polyneices. Tragedy drove Oedipus from the land, and Thebes was left without a ruler. The citizens of Thebes held an election and chose Eteocles to be king.

Polyneices believed that since he was the older brother it was his right to rule the land. The two brothers quarreled and Eteocles banished Polyneices, who pledged revenge.Polyneices left Thebes and gathered a large army to fight for the throne.

　　公民的不服从是一种只有在似乎已经没有其他可选方法的情况下才能做出的极端选择。什么时候它会转变成为适当的选择？在这一课里，你们将思考挑战权威的限度。虽然你们可能永远不会从事公民不服从的行为，但你们仍然有可能会遇到违背了你们的道德或宗教原则的法律。以下练习将帮助你们思考，在这种情况下你们应该考虑什么，它会成为你解决这一棘手问题的工具。

重点思考练习

对安提戈涅的故事中描述的公民不服从权利发表你的看法

　　阅读下面的故事，然后按照提示准备一场班级辩论。

　　故事改编自索福克勒斯写于公元前 442 年的希腊悲剧《安提戈涅》，它讲述了一个年轻女人安提戈涅为顺应自己良心的指引而触犯法律并接受惩罚的故事。

《安提戈涅的悲剧》

　　在安提戈涅18岁的时候，她的叔父克瑞翁成为了古希腊一座重要的城市——底比斯城的统治者。安提戈涅和克瑞翁都是意志坚定的人，他们都深信自己的思想是正确的，谁也不愿向对方屈服，也因此给他们自己和这座城市都带来了巨大的灾难。

　　何时反抗政治权威才是正确的？安提戈涅从自己的个人感情出发回答了这个问题，并因此而献出生命。克瑞翁对此有不同的答案，却也因此失去了他深爱的一切。

克瑞翁的命令

　　在克瑞翁之前，他的兄长俄狄浦斯是底比斯城的统治者。俄狄浦斯有两个女儿——安提戈涅和伊斯墨涅，以及两个儿子——厄忒俄克勒斯和波吕尼刻斯。弑父娶母的悲剧迫使俄狄浦斯远走他乡，底比斯城一时变成无主之城，公民们于是选举了厄忒俄克勒斯为国王。

　　波吕尼刻斯认为，既然他是长兄，理应是由他来统治。兄弟俩争吵了一番，厄忒俄克勒斯将波吕尼刻斯驱逐出境。波吕尼刻斯为此发誓报仇。他离开底比斯城后召集了庞大的军队为争夺王位而战。

Polyneices and his army returned to Thebes and waged a fierce attack against the city. It was a long and bitter civil war, with brother fighting against brother. During the course of the war, many died and much property was destroyed. Finally, Polyneices and Eteocles fought and killed each other.

Once again, the people of Thebes were without a ruler. So they elected Creon king. Creon spoke to the people and reminded them about what happened when authority was ignored. He told them that for good of their land, they must learn from this sad time. As an example, he decreed that Eteocles was to receive a hero's funeral, while Polyneices, who fought against Thebes, was to rot on the field of battle. No person could erect a gravestone in Polyneices' memory; no person could mourn for him. Any person who disobeyed this decree and buried Polyneices's body would be put to death.

The people of Thebes debated the wisdom of Creon's decree. On one side, many believed it was a sacred duty to bury the dead. According to their beliefs, unburied souls were doomed to wander alone throughout eternity. Others believed that Creon's decree was justified because the city had suffered from rebels and lawbreakers. Polyneices's fate would serve as an example to those who did not respect the authority of the state.

A Higher Law

Antigone, Polyneices's sister, passionately believed that the laws of the gods were higher and more important than the laws of the state. She intended to follow the laws of the gods and bury her brother. Antigone attempted to convince Ismene to join her.

"Do you mean to bury our brother's body, Antigone, when it is forbidden by law?" Ismene asked her sister.

"If you will not join me, I will do your share too," Antigone replied. "I will never be false to my brother!"

"Are you not going too far, exceeding the limits," Ismene asked, "when you do what Creon, who is the king, has forbidden?"

"He has no right to keep me from observing sacred custom." Antigone spoke with great firmness.

波吕尼刻斯和他的军队回到了底比斯城，并对城邦发起了激烈的攻击。这场兄弟之间的自相残杀艰难且漫长。在战争中许多人失去生命，许多财富被摧毁。最终两兄弟在面对面的对决中同归于尽。

底比斯人再一次失去了统治者，随后他们选择了克瑞翁为国王。克瑞翁对人民发表了演讲，并提醒他们，当权威被忽视的时候将发生怎样悲惨的事情。他告诉人们，为了守护自己的土地，他们必须从这一悲伤的时刻吸取教训。为树立典范，克瑞翁下令为厄忒俄克勒斯举行了英雄般的葬礼，而反攻底比斯城的波吕尼刻斯的尸体要被丢在战场上腐烂，任何人都不许为波吕尼刻斯立碑，不能为他哀悼，任何不遵守该命令并埋葬波吕尼刻斯尸体的人都将被处以死刑。

底比斯人民对克瑞翁的法令展开了辩论，许多人认为埋葬死者是一种神圣的职责。根据他们的信仰，不被掩埋的灵魂注定要成为孤魂野鬼，永远在外游荡。而其他人认为，克瑞翁的法令是有道理的，因为这个城市由于叛乱和违法者而备受折磨，波吕尼克斯的下场可以作为教育那些不尊重国家权威的人的实例。

更高的法律

波吕尼克斯的妹妹安提戈涅虔诚地相信神的法律高于国家的法律，且比国家的法律更重要，她打算遵照神的法律埋葬她的哥哥。安提戈涅试图说服她的妹妹伊斯墨涅和她一起完成这件事。

"安提戈涅你是说，法律禁止任何人埋葬我们的哥哥，你却要这么做吗？" 伊斯墨涅问她的姐姐。

"如果你不帮忙，我也要替你对哥哥尽义务，"安提戈涅说："我永远不会背弃哥哥。"

"在克瑞翁国王颁布禁令之后公然触犯它？这样超越限制难道不是有点过头了吗？"伊斯墨涅问。

安提戈涅坚定地回答："他没有权利阻止我遵从神圣的习俗。"

"If we do as you wish and defy the law," Ismene continued, "we will find ourselves alone against the powers of the king and we will perish! Since we are forced to obey this law, we can ask the gods' forgiveness. "

"Obey the law if you must, Ismene," said Antigone. "I will not urge you further to join me. But I will bury Polyneices without your help. If I am killed because of it, then so be it. My 'crime' will be no sin, for I owe a greater allegiance to the laws made by the gods than I do to those made by man. If you do not join me in my action, you will be guilty of dishonoring the gods' laws."

"I have no wish to dishonor the gods' laws, Antigone," Ismene replied, "but I have no strength to defy the state." "Then I will act alone to honor the brother I love," Antigone said.

Punishment

As Antigone went to bury her brother, Creon entered the garden with two attendants. He was deeply worried about the decision he had just made.

"It is our loyalty to the state that is the highest good. Those who look on their friends or family as of greater worth than their city are wrong. They forget that it is the ship of state that carries us safely through life's stormy voyage and only while she prospers can we make true friends or live decently at all. Worse are those like my nephew Polyneices who turn against their own land and make war against it. No honor shall be given to them.

'These are my rules! That is why my edict honors all those who died in battle fighting for our city but forbids touching Polyneices, who made war against his own land. He tried to taste the blood of his own kin and make slaves of all the others; his body shall be left untouched, unmourned, and unburied as a mark of shame and dishonor. Only by these rules can our city be safe and prosper. Only by obedience to them can this city avoid civil war and ruin."

Suddenly, a guard burst into the garden and brought news that Polyneices had been buried. Creon angrily gave orders to find the guilty person. The guard returned with Antigone in custody.

"I caught this woman in the act of burying the body of Polyneices."

"如果我们像你所说的那样触犯法律"，伊斯墨涅接着说："到时会发现只有我们两个反抗国王的权力，我们将会受到重罚！因为我们是被迫服从这道命令的，我们可以祈求上天的原谅。"

"如果你必须要遵守法律那就这么做吧，伊斯墨涅，"安提戈涅说："我再也不求你加入了，我要独自埋葬哥哥。即使为此而死也是件光荣的事，我的"罪行"将不是真的罪过，我更效忠于上帝制定而非人定的法律。如果你不加入我的行动，那么你将会为藐视上帝的法律而感到羞耻。"

"我并不藐视上帝的法律，安提戈涅，"伊斯墨涅回答："我只是没有力量和城邦对抗。"

"那么我现在要独自去纪念我最亲爱的兄长。"安提戈涅说。

惩罚

当安提戈涅埋葬她的哥哥时，克瑞翁与两个随从走进花园，他正在为自己刚做的决定而感到十分忧虑。

"我们对国家的忠诚就是最高的善，那些把他们的朋友或家人看得比自己的城邦更重要的人是错误的。他们忘记了正是国家这艘船搭载着我们安全地渡过了人生的风雨航程，而也只有国家繁荣幸福才能让我们交到真正的朋友，生活得更体面。更糟糕的就是像我的侄子波吕尼克斯这样的人，背叛自己的家园，转头就向自己的国家宣战的人，就不应该给予他们任何荣誉。"

"这就是我的规矩！这就是为什么我的政令敬重那些为我们的城市奋战，牺牲在战场上的人，但禁止任何人接近波吕尼克斯这个向自己的国家宣战的人。他想喝他自己族人的血，让所有其他人都成为奴隶；他的尸体就应该暴露在荒野，作为羞愧和耻辱的标记，不许人接近，不许人哀悼，也不许人埋葬。只有通过这些规则，我们的城邦才能是安全和繁荣的；只有通过服从这些规则，才能使这座城邦避免内战和毁灭。"

突然，一名卫兵跑进花园，报告了波吕尼刻斯的尸体已经被埋葬的消息，克瑞翁愤怒地下令找出嫌犯。卫兵将安提戈涅带回来，并羁押审问了她："我抓住了这个女人时，她正在埋葬波吕尼刻斯的尸体。"

Creon turned to his niece Antigone and asked if she denied trying to bury Polyneices's body. She did not deny it.

Creon now said to Antigone, "Tell me, did you not know that there is a law forbidding what you did; and if you did know, why did you disobey it? You are my niece and are soon to marry my son, Haemon. How can this be?"

"I knew the law," Antigone answered. "It was public knowledge. As for why I did it, hear this: It was not Zeus, king of the gods, who published that edict. Your law is not part of eternal justice, and I do not believe that your laws always compel me to obey. The unwritten laws of eternal justice are a higher law and in their name I disobeyed your lesser law.

"Your law is the law of today," she continued, "but the laws of heaven are for eternity, for all times and all places. No one even knows when they were first put forth. Eternal law commands that I bury my brother, Polyneices. I will die for doing so, but I would die someday in any case. Being put to death by you is of no importance to me. If I had allowed my brother to lie untouched, unburied, and uncared for, that would have disturbed me deeply. I am therefore not sorry for what I did."

'This brother of yours was attacking his own state!" Creon retorted. "There is no glory in aiding those who make treasonous attack on your own country, which ought to hold your highest loyalty and allegiance. What of your other brother, who died defending the state?"

"Nevertheless, the gods require what I have done," said Antigone. "In honoring the dead I follow a higher law than the law of the state. What is more, my fellow The beans agree with me, only fear seals their lips." 'The gods require no loyalty to such evil doers," said Creon.

"You cannot speak for the gods. Who can say that they don't agree with me?" replied Antigone. "It is my duty to produce order and peace in this war-torn land," Creon went on. "Our city is still in danger, divided between the supporters of both your dead brothers. The fate of the rebel Polyneices must serve as a warning to all those who would disobey the laws and overthrow the state.

克瑞翁看着他的侄女安提戈涅，并问她是否真的埋葬了波吕尼刻斯的尸体。她并不否认。

克雷翁对安提戈涅说："告诉我，你是不是不知道有法规禁止你做这件事？如果你确实知道，又为什么不遵守呢？你是我的侄女，不久就要与我的儿子海蒙结婚。事情怎么会变成这样呢？"

"我了解法律，"安提戈涅回答："但这是公共知识。至于我为什么知道了还这么做，因为这不是众神之王宙斯颁布的法令。你的法律不属于永恒的正义，我不相信你的法律能总是让我服从，代表永恒正义的不成文法律才是更高的法律，以它们的名义，我不会服从于你的法律，因为那跟神的法律相比更次要。"

"你的法是当今的法律，"她接着说："但上天的法律在任何时候、任何地方都是永恒的。甚至没有人知道神明在什么时候订立了这些法律。永恒的法律命令我埋葬我的哥哥波吕尼克斯。我知道会为了这件事而死去，但总有一天我会死，你下令处死我对我来说一点也不重要。如果我让我的哥哥躺在野外，没有人触摸，没有人掩埋，没有人关心，这将会使我深深地不安和难过，因此我不后悔我所做的事。"

"可是你的这位哥哥攻打他自己的国家！"克雷翁反驳道："帮助那些转过头来攻打自己的国家的叛徒是不光彩的，他本应该对国家保持最高忠诚和并时刻效忠，如此的话，誓死保卫国家的你的弟弟呢？"

"但是，是神明要求我这么做的，"安提戈涅说："在纪念故人的事情上，我遵循一种高于国家法律的更高法。更重要的是，我的同胞底比斯人也同意我的看法，只是恐惧你封住了他们的嘴。"

"众神不需要像你这种做出邪恶行为的人的忠诚。"克瑞翁说。

"你不能代表神明发言。谁可以说他们不同意我的看法？"安提戈涅回答。

"我的职责就是在这片饱受战争蹂躏的土地上建立秩序与和平，"克瑞翁继续说："我们的城市仍然处于危险之中，因为你两个兄弟的不同支持者而处于分裂状态。叛乱的波吕尼克斯的命运必须作为对那些触犯法律，推翻国家的人的一种警告。"

"You have thrown away your future happiness to bury one rebellious brother, Antigone. In disobeying the law on which the safety and well-being of the whole city depends, you make it impossible for me to avoid putting you to death.

"Antigone, it is my belief that a single unburied corpse is a fair payment for restoring peace and order to Thebes, but you refuse to accept that. So be it. You leave me no choice. Guards, take this woman from my sight and lock her away! She must not escape from her appointment with death!"

Haemon's Appeal

When Haemon, Antigone's fiance, heard what had happened, he went to his father Creon to beg for a pardon. Creon refused.

"Of all citizens of Thebes, I have found Antigone and Antigone alone disobedient to my law," Creon explained to Haemon. "If I do not kill her, I will look like a liar to my own people. The citizens of Thebes will think me weak. The public order, the state itself will be in jeopardy. I cannot have two rules, one for my kin and another for everyone else.

"My son, if this city is to survive, authority must be obeyed in small as well as great matters, even in unjust as well as just things. Disobedience is the worst of evils. It ruins cities. It makes wastelands out of homes."

After hearing his father speak, Haemon answered, "Father, hear me out. Far be it from me to say you are not right. Yet others-even I-may also have useful thoughts. I am your eyes and ears, and I can tell you what citizens fear to tell you to your face. Father, they are talking. I hear people murmuring in the dark; they are moaning for Antigone. They say she deserves reward not punishment for what she has done. Such is the dark rumor that spreads in secret.

"Those who are truly wise must know that there is a time to bend and not insist on their will. Don't you see, father, when the wind blows fiercely, the trees that yield to it save every twig, while the stiff and unbending perish root and branch? Spare Antigone, for if you kill her the people will turn against you."

"安提戈涅，你抛弃了你未来的幸福去埋葬你的叛徒哥哥。由于你不遵守整个城邦的安全和福祉仰赖的法律，我无法不处以你死刑。"

"安提戈涅，我相信，一个不被掩埋的尸体就是恢复底比斯的和平与秩序所必须付出的公平的代价，但是你拒绝接受这一点。就这样吧。你要离开我别无选择。警卫，把这个女人带走，把她关进监狱！她免不了一死！"

海蒙的申诉

当安提戈涅的未婚夫海蒙听说刚刚发生的事情后，找到他的父亲克瑞翁，请求他的原谅。克瑞翁拒绝了。

"我发现，所有底比斯的公民中只有安提戈涅不服从我的法律"，克瑞翁向海蒙解释："如果我不杀她，我在自己的人民面前会像一个骗子。底比斯的公民会认为我软弱，公共秩序和国家本身都将处于危险之中，我不能同时拥有两个规则，一个适用于我的亲人，另一个给其他所有人。"

"我的儿子，如果城邦要为了生存，无论事务大小，无论事情是否公平，都必须服从权威。不服从是最大的恶，它摧毁城市，让我们的家园变得荒芜。"

听了他父亲的话，海蒙回答："爸爸，请听我说完。我没有资格来说你是错误的。然而，其他人（甚至是我）可能也会有有益的想法。我是你的眼睛和耳朵，我可以告诉你那些公民害怕当面跟你说的话。父亲，他们在说。我听到人们在黑暗中窃窃私语，他们为安提戈涅哀悼，他们说她所做的事情值得被奖励而不是惩罚，这就是暗中传播的谣言。"

"真正聪明的人必须知道每个人都要学会妥协，而不是一味坚持自己的意志。父亲，难道你没有看到，猛烈的大风刮起时，只有那些屈服于风的树木才能保护自己的每一根枝条，而僵硬顽固的树连则要根茎都要被大风拔起吗？释放安提戈涅吧，如果你杀了她，人民将会转而反对你。"

"Is it your wish that I honor lawlessness?" asked Creon, "For that is what Antigone represents. Should I show respect for evil doers?" Said Haemon, 'The people of Thebes with one voice deny that Antigone is evil. You have no authority, father, to disobey the gods' requirements The gods have their own laws, superior to yours."

"Don't talk to me about laws, Haemon. The laws of this world hold together our city, our civilization. Civil war has torn apart our city. Our wounds are fresh and still unhealed. If Antigone has her way, it will mean that anyone can disobey whatever laws they decide are wrong. If those who break the law go unpunished, our fragile civic order will be reduced to chaos. Even the innocent will suffer! We will be a lawless city, no different from barbarians."

Tragic Consequences

Creon ordered Antigone taken to a cave and abandoned. On the road to the cave that would be both prison and tomb, Antigone spoke to the crowd who had gathered to see her.

 What might be the consequences of allowing Antigone to go unpunished for disobeying the laws of the state? ☞

"难道你希望我尊敬毫无法纪的人？"克瑞翁问："这就是安提戈涅所代表的人，我应该尊敬做出邪恶行为的人吗？"海蒙说："底比斯人都异口同声地否认安提戈涅是邪恶的，父亲，你没有权威违抗神明的要求，众神有自己的法律，要高于您的。"

"不要跟我谈论法律，海蒙，这个世界的法律把我们的城邦、我们的文明紧紧团结在一起，内战撕裂了我们的城市，我们尚未愈合的伤口还在淌血，如果安提戈涅有她自己的方式，这将意味着任何人都可以违抗任何他们认为是错误的法律。如果那些违法的人被赦免、逍遥法外，那么我们脆弱的城邦秩序将消失殆尽，陷入一片混乱。即便是无辜的人都要遭殃！我们的城邦将无法可依，就像从前的野蛮时期一样。"

悲惨的结局

克瑞翁下令把安提戈涅带到一个山洞并被抛弃。在去山洞（既是监狱也是坟墓）的路上，安提戈涅向聚拢在她身边的人群说：

如果赦免安提戈涅触犯城邦法律的罪行，让她免受惩罚，会有什么结果？

"See me, people of Thebes, citizens of my homeland," she called out. "See me setting out on my last journey, looking at sunlight for the last time. I will die unwed, unmourned, and friendless. What a miserable creature I am! As night follows the day, the fate I cannot escape has overtaken me. Why am I to die?"

Creon entered from the palace and said, "Citizens of Thebes, hear what I have to say. It is a sad command that I give, but one that I must. Antigone has knowingly defied the law of the state by attempting to bury Polyneices. "If we allow people to defy the law," he continued, "our city will not survive. It is my duty, my solemn obligation as ruler, not to allow our city to be threatened by such a rebellious act. Antigone will therefore be taken to the mountain and imprisoned in a cave. Food will be left for her, but only enough to protect the reputation of Thebes against an accusation of excessive cruelty."

He turned to the woman before him and said, "Do you, Antigone, have any final words? "

"Only this, Creon. I am being sent to my death because I have chosen to obey the laws of heaven rather than those of earth. I know my reverence for the gods has offended you, but in my own mind and heart I feel I have not sinned; I have committed no crime. I have done no more than my duty. I will trust myself to the gods I have served, knowing that I have disobeyed no laws of theirs."

After the guards took Antigone away, a blind prophet warned Creon against putting Antigone to death. "The sun's chariot will race scarcely once across the sky before you pay for Antigone's fate with a corpse of your own flesh. Soon your house will be filled with wailing. You shall not escape my prophecy!"

If you were Creon, what questions might you ask in deciding whether to punish Antigone? ☞

"看着我，底比斯人，我祖国的公民！"她喊道："看着我迈向我最后的旅程，看着我最后一次望向阳光。我即将死去，没有结婚，无人哀悼，没有朋友。我是多么可怜！就像白天之后是夜晚一般，我无法逃避的命运压倒了我。为什么我会死？"

克瑞翁走上宫殿说："底比斯的公民，请听我说，这是我做出的一个令人悲伤却不得不这样做的决定。安提戈涅明知故犯，企图埋葬波吕尼克斯，触犯了国家的法律。"

"如果我们允许人们以身试法，"他继续说："我们的城邦将无法生存下去。这是我的责任，我作为统治者的庄严义务，不能让我们的城市因为这样的背叛行为而受到威胁。安提戈涅将因此被带到山上，囚禁在一个山洞里，会为她留下食物，但只能满足维护底比斯声誉的需要，以回应公民说我过分残酷的指责。"

他转向他面前的女人说："你，安提戈涅，有没有什么最后的话要说？"

"只有如此，克瑞翁，因为我选择了服从上帝的不是凡人的法律而被赐死。我知道我对神明的崇敬冒犯了你，但在我自己的心灵和思想里，我觉得自己没有犯罪，我不过是是履行了自己的责任。我会将我托付给我所信仰的神，他们知道我没有违背他们的法律。"

在警卫带走安提戈涅后，一个反对赐安提戈涅死刑的盲人先知警告克瑞翁说："太阳的战车还没在天空中走完一圈，你就会为安提戈涅的死付出一具来自你的肉体的尸体的代价，很快你的房子将充满哀号，你将无法逃过我的预言！"

如果你是克瑞翁，在考虑是否惩罚安提戈涅时你会问什么问题？

Finally, with great reluctance, Creon agreed to reverse his decision. It was too late. As he approached the prison cave, he heard his son Haemon's voice grieving for his beloved Antigone, who had hanged herself.

Looking in the cave, Creon saw his son weeping with his arms around his would-be bride. Creon begged his son to come away. But Haernon screamed curses at him and stabbed herself to death, clinging to Antigone in his last dying moments.

Not many hours later, a messenger arrived to tell Creon that the dimensions of the tragedy were even greater than he knew. When his wife heard of Haemon's death, she too took her life. Creon's life was in ruins. All that he loved was gone. He became a broken man longing for nothing more than the release of death.

Preparing for a Class Debate

Your teacher will divide your class into five groups:

- Group 1 will develop and present initial arguments for Creon's position.

- Group 2 will develop and present rebuttal arguments responding to the arguments made for Antigone's position.

- Group 3 will develop and present initial arguments for Antigone's position.

- Group 4 will develop and present rebuttal arguments responding to the arguments made for Creon's position.

- Group 5 will represent the citizens of Thebes, who will listen to the presentations of both sides, ask questions, and decide which groups have presented the better arguments.

Each group should follow the instructions below in preparing for the debate.

Group 1: Creon

Your group will defend Creon's position. Prepare your arguments and select spokespersons to present your arguments to the class.

最后，克瑞翁极不情愿地同意推翻自己的决定。但为时已晚，当他走近监狱洞穴时听到了他的儿子海蒙悲痛欲绝的声音，哀悼着上吊自杀的他的挚爱——安提戈涅。

克瑞翁朝洞里看过去，看到他的儿子双臂拥着他的未婚妻。克瑞翁恳求他的儿子离开这里。但海蒙尖叫着诅咒他，然后用刀刺死了自己，奄奄一息的时刻也一直陪在安提戈涅身边。

数小时后，一个信使告诉克瑞翁，悲剧比他所知道的还要多：当克瑞翁的妻子听说了儿子海蒙死后，也结束了自己的生命。克瑞翁的生活崩塌了，他所挚爱的一切都离他远去，他成了一个除了渴望死亡之外其他什么都不想要的绝望的人。

准备课堂辩论：

老师会把你们全班分成以下五个小组：
- 第一组将提出和陈述支持克瑞翁观点的初始论据
- 第二组将提出和陈述反驳论据，用来回应支持安提戈涅观点的论据
- 第三组将提出和陈述支持安提戈涅观点的初始论据
- 第四组将提出和陈述反驳论据，用来回应支持克瑞翁观点的论据
- 第五组将代表底比斯公民，听取双方的陈述，提出质询，并判断哪一组陈述的论据更好

每组都应遵循以下说明准备辩论：

第一组：克瑞翁小组

你们组将为克瑞翁的观点进行辩护。准备你们的论据，并选出发言人向全班陈述你们的论据。

Group 2: Creon's rebuttal

Your group will respond to the arguments made for Antigone's position. Anticipate what those arguments will be, prepare your rebuttal arguments, and select spokespersons to present your rebuttal argument to the class.

Group 3: Antigone

Your group will defend Antigone's position. Prepare your arguments and select spokespersons to present your arguments to the class.

Group 4: Antigone's rebuttal

Your group will respond to the arguments made for Creon's position. Anticipate what those arguments will be, prepare your rebuttal arguments and select spokespersons to present your rebuttal arguments to the class.

Group 5: Citizens of Thebes

Your group will represent the citizens of Thebes. You will question all the above groups to decide whose position you prefer. Select a chairperson for your group. Develop a list of questions to evaluate the positions of the other groups and to challenge their arguments.

Coucting the Class Debate

1. After all groups have had time to prepare, the chairperson of the citizens' group should call the debate fo order.

2. Each group will have five minutes to make its presentations, the order will be Group 1, Group 3, Group 4, Group 2. After each presentation, citizens of Thebes may ask questions.

3. Members of the group making the presentation may consult with each other before answering questions. Any member of the group may answer a question.

4. After each group has presented its arguments and answered questions, the citizens' group should meet to decide who made the most persuasive arguments. The chairperson should explain the group's decision to the class. The class should then discuss the decision of the citizens' group and answer the What do you think? questions on the next page.

第二组：克瑞翁的反驳论据小组

你们组将对证明安提戈涅观点的论据做出回应。预估对方可能提出的论据，准备你们的反驳论据，选出发言人向全班陈述你们的反驳论据。

第三组：安提戈涅小组

你们组将为安提戈涅的观点进行辩护。准备你们的论据，并选出发言人向全班陈述你们的论据。

第四组：安提戈涅的反驳论据小组

你们组将对证明克瑞翁观点的论据做出回应。预估对方可能提出的论据，准备你们的反驳论据，选出发言人向全班陈述你们的反驳论据。

第五组：底比斯公民小组

你们组将代表底比斯的公民。你们将质询上述所有小组，并选出你们支持哪种观点。

请为你们的小组选出一位主席。列出一个问题集，用来评估其他各组的观点，并对他们的论据提出质疑。

进行课堂辩论

1. 在各组有充足时间做好准备后，公民小组主持人应当宣布辩论开始。

2. 每个小组都有 5 分钟时间做陈述发言，发言顺序应当是：第一组、第三组、第四组、第二组。每个小组发言结束后，底比斯公民可以提问。

3. 小组成员当中发表陈述的代表在回答问题之前可以向其他小组成员征询意见。小组中的任何成员都可以回答一个问题。

4. 在各组发表了自己的论据并回答完问题后，公民小组应当开会决定哪一组的论据最有说服力。主席应当向全班解释该组的决定。随后全班应讨论公民小组的决议，并回答下一页中"你怎么看？"部分的问题。

What do you think?

I. What were the strengths and weaknesses of Creon's position? Of Antigone's?

2. Were there other effective ways for Antigone to protest Creon's law? If so, what were they?

3. What factors should be considered in deciding to disobey a law?

4. What if people of different religious or moral values disagree about the meaning of the higher law?

5. Do you think civil disobedience is ever justified? Explain your position.

Using the Lesson

1. Many states, including Michigan, have laws which prohibit assisting in suicide attempts. Dr. Jack Kevorkian openly violated Michigan's law, claiming that a higher law-the Constitution gave people the right to end their own lives, and to have the assistance of a doctor in order to do so. Do research to find out what happened to Dr. Kevorkian, and report to the class what you learn.

2. During World War II, many people risked their lives by disobeying Nazi laws that required Jews to surrender themselves for deportation. For example, in Chambon-sur-Lignon, a village in the south of France, the entire town provided hiding places for Jewish refugees. In Denmark, leaders such as King Christian X and the Lutheran Bishop of Copenhagen publicly opposed the Nazi deportation laws, and with the crucial assistance of non-Jewish Danes more than nine-tenths of the Jewish population managed to escape to Sweden. Working with a group of classmates, do library research to learn more about these or other efforts to resist unjust Nazi laws, and prepare a skit to dramatize what happened. Perform your skit for the class, and then discuss the issues of authority that are involved.

你怎么看?

1. 克瑞翁的观点有哪些优势和劣势? 安提戈涅的观点有哪些优势和劣势?

2. 安提戈涅反抗克瑞翁的法律是否有其他有效方法? 如果有, 是什么?

3. 决定不服从法律时应当考虑什么因素?

4. 如果不同宗教或道德价值观的人不同意最高法的定义该怎么办?

5. 你认为公民的不服从是永远合理的吗? 解释你的观点。

知识运用

1. 美国的许多州(包括密歇根州),都设有法律禁止协助任何自杀企图。杰克凯佛基安博士公开违反密歇根州的法律,声称更高法——宪法赋予了人民结束自己生命的权利,并有权得到医生的协助。研究这个案例,探寻发生在凯佛基安博士身上的事情经过,并向全班报告你的所学。

2. 二战期间,有许多人冒着生命危险,违背纳粹要求驱逐犹太人的法律。例如,在法国南部小镇:勒尚邦利尼翁(Chambon-sur-Lignon),整个村镇都为犹太难民提供了藏身之地。在丹麦,国王克里斯蒂安十世和哥本哈根路德教会的主教都公开反对纳粹驱逐犹太人的法律。在非犹太裔的丹麦人的大力援助下,有超过十分之九的犹太居民设法逃往瑞典。与小组同学合作,到图书馆调查并进一步了解其他诸如此类抵制不正义的纳粹法律的案例,并排练一个短剧来描述这类事件的经过。在班上表演你们的短剧,然后讨论剧中所包含的权威问题。

附录1:
词汇表

abolitionist AL4. A person who advocated the end of slavery in the United States.

废奴主义者（《权威》第四课）：在美国支持废除奴隶制的人。

accountable AL8 (accountability). Obliged to answer for one's actions.

负责任的（《权威》第八课）：有义务为某人的行为负责。

aristocracy AL2. A governing body or upper class usually made up of an hereditary nobility.

贵族（《权威》第二课）：通常由世袭贵族组成的统治团体或上层阶级。

authority AL1. The rules or the people who govern our lives; the power to influence or command thought, opinion, or behavior.

权威（《权威》第一课）：管理（或支配）我们生活的规则或人；影响（或指挥）人们的思想、观点或行为的力量。

bailiff AL9. A minor official who guards prisoners and maintains order in a courtroom.

法警（《权威》第九课）：在法庭看管囚犯和维持秩序的警官。

bill AL7. A proposed law presented to a legislature.

提案（《权威》第七课）：提交立法机关审议的法律议案。

Bill of Rights AL8, AL14. The first ten amendments to the U.S. Constitution, a summary of fundamental rights and privileges guaranteed to a people against violation by the state.

《权利法案》（《权威》第八课、第十四课）：美国宪法的前十项修正案，是对保障人民反抗政府干预的基本权利和特权的总结。

blockade AL12. The closing off of a city or harbor by troops or warships to prevent people and supplies from going in or out.

封锁（《权威》第十二课）：用军队或战舰封闭某座城市或港口，阻断人员和物资进出。

characteristics AL6. Distinguishing traits, qualities, or properties.

特性（《权威》第六课）：与众不同的、显著的特点、特质或属性。

civil disobedience AL14. Violating a law or protesting a government policy on the grounds that the law or policy is morally unjust.

公民的不服从（《权威》第十四课）：由于某项法规或政府的政策在道德上是不公正的，公民拒绝遵守这项法律或反对这项政策。

conscience AL2. Fundamental ideas about right and wrong that come from religion, ethics, and individual morality; the sense or consciousness of the moral goodness or blameworthiness of one's own conduct, intentions, or character together with a feeling of obligation to do right or be good.

良知（《权威》第二课）：来源于宗教、伦理和个人道德的一些基本的是非观念；基于一种"要做正确的事"或"要做一个好人"的责任感，而对个人的行为、动机或个性中的道德良善或应受谴责之处的观念或意识。

consent AL2. Agreement as to action or opinion.

同意（《权威》第二课）：对行为或观点的赞同。

criteria AL6. Characterizing marks or traits; a standard on which a judgment or decision may be based.

标准（《权威》第六课）：赋予显著特性的标志或特点；为做出某种判断或决定可依据的准则。

custom AL2. Long-established practice considered as unwritten law; the whole body of usages, practices, and conventions that regulate social life.

习俗（《权威》第二课）：（人们）视之为不成文法的长期确立的习惯；影响和控制社会生活的习惯、惯例与传统的。

dilemma AL12. A situation involving a choice between two equally unsatisfactory alternatives.

困境（《权威》第十二课）：涉及到需要在两个同样不足的选项中做出选择的状况。

diligence AL4. Steady, earnest, and energetic effort.

勤奋（《权威》第四课）：持续的、非常认真的以及积极的努力。

divine right AL2. The belief that God granted to those of royal birth the right to rule their people.

神授的权利（《权威》第二课）：相信上帝授予了那些拥有皇家血统的人以统治其臣民的权利。

duties AL4. Actions required of someone by position, social custom, law, or religion.

职责（《权威》第四课）：由身份地位、社会习俗、法律或宗教所决定的个体行为。

economic costs AL8. The expense of supporting institutions or gaining benefits.

经济成本（《权威》第八课）：维护机构或获得收益所需的花销。

efficiency AL8. Effective operation as measured by comparing production with cost-as in energy, time, and money.

效率（《权威》第八课）：通过生产与成本之间比较，并以能源、时间和金钱来衡量的有效运营。

endangered species AL7. A group of biologically similar animals or plants that are threatened with distinction.

濒危物种（《权威》第七课）：濒临灭绝威胁的一组生物上近似的动物或植物。

espionage AL12. The practice of spying or use of spies to obtain information about the plans and activities of a foreign government.

间谍（《权威》第十二课）：从事秘密侦察活动，或用间谍来获取某外国政府的计划或行动的情报。

extinct. AL7 No longer existing.

灭绝（《权威》第七课）：不再存在。

flogging AL11. Beating with a rod or whip.

鞭刑（《权威》第十一课）：用鞭子抽打。

heredity AL2 (hereditary). The passage of traits from parents to offspring; genetic transmission.

世袭、遗传（《权威》第二课）：某些特性从父母到子孙后代的传递路径；基因传递。

higher law AL14. As used in describing a legal system, refers to the superiority of one set of laws over another. For example, the U.S. Constitution is a higher law than any federal or state law. In the natural rights philosophy, it means that natural law and divine law are superior to laws made by human beings.

更高的法律（《权威》第十四课）：用于描述某一种法律体系，特指某一种法律凌驾于另一种法律之上。例如，美国宪法对于其他联邦或各州法律来说是一种"更高的法律"。在自然权利哲学里，它意味着自然法和神的法高于人类所制定的各项法律。

humane AL10. Marked by compassion, sympathy, or consideration for human beings or animals.

人道（《权威》第十课）：对人类或动物的怜悯与同情，或为人类或动物考虑。

hypothetical AL6/13. Presumed; based on supposition.

假设（《权威》第六课、第十三课）：假定、假如；基于某种猜测。

inaccessibility AL8. State of being unapproachable.

难以接近（《权威》第八课）：无法接近的状态（样子）。

incompetent (incompetence AL8). Lacking adequate ability or qualities.

无能（《权威》第八课）：缺乏足够的能力或资质。

institution AL2. An established practice, custom, or pattern of behavior important in the cultural life of a society.

机构、制度（《权威》第二课）：在某一社会的文化生活中具有重要意义的一套既定的实践、习俗或行为模式。

internment camp AL12. A place where people are detained, especially during wartime.

集中营（《权威》第十二课）：特指在战争时期人们被集中扣押的地方。

kangaroo court AL1. A mock court in which the principles of law and justice are disregarded or perverted.

私设法庭（《权威》第一课）：法律和正义的准则被忽视或扭曲的模拟（伪）法庭。

levy (taxes) AL5. To impose or collect monies by legal authority.

征收（税款）（《权威》第五课）：由合法权威实施或收取的费用。

limit AL10. Something that restricts or keeps in bounds.

限制（《权威》第十课）：使受到限制或保持在规定范围内。

monarchy AL2. Undivided rule or absolute sovereignty by a single person; a government having an hereditary chief of state with life tenure.

君主（《权威》第二课）：由单一个人拥有的不可分割的治权或绝对主权。

paramilitary AL1. Organized to imitate a military unit but outside of the regular military forces.

半军事化（《权威》第一课）：正规军事力量之外有组织的模拟军事单位

penalty AL14. A disadvantage, loss, or hardship established by law or authority for a crime, action, or offense.

惩罚（《权威》第十四课）：法律或权威针对某种犯罪、行动或触犯法律的行为所设定的不利后果、损失和苦难。

pollution AL5. The contamination of air, water, or land by harmful substances.

污染（《权威》第五课）：空气、水或土地被有毒物质污染。

position of authority AL4. A role giving the person who fills it the power to influence thought, opinion, or behavior.

权威职位（《权威》第四课）：某种职能，担当该职能的人同时被赋予了影响思想、观点或行为的权力。

power AL1. The ability to control or direct something or someone; possession of control, authority, or influence over others.

权力（《权威》第一课）：控制或命令某事或某人的能力；拥有对他人的控制、权威或影响力。

privileges AL4. Rights granted as benefits, advantages, or favors.

特权（《权威》第四课）：作为利益、优势或恩惠而被特许赋予的权利。

proclamation AL12. An official, formal, public announcement.

公告（《权威》第十二课）：一种官方的、正式的、公开的宣告。

public defender AL9. A lawyer whose duty is to defend accused persons unable to pay for legal assistance.

公设辩护律师（《权威》第九课）：为无法支付辩护费用的被告人提供法律援助的律师。

qualifications AL4. Qualities or skills which suit a person to a specific position.

资格（《权威》第四课）：某个人适合担任某个特定职位的资质或技能。

role AL2. The proper function of a person; characteristics and expected behavior of individuals.

职能（《权威》第二课）：某个人的特定职责与能力；个人的典型特征和预定（expected）行为。

sabotage AL12. The deliberate destruction of property or disruption of work by enemy agents or resistance fighters in wartime.

蓄意破坏（《权威》第十二课）：战争时期敌方情报人员或抵抗组织战士故意破坏财物或阻断工作进程的行为。

scope AL10. The range of one's perceptions, thoughts, actions, or abilities; the area covered by an activity.

范围（《权威》第十课）：一个人的理解、思想、行为或能力的范畴；能力所及的领域。

secede AL12. To withdraw from a federation

脱离（《权威》第十二课）：从某个联盟（联邦）中退出。

source of authority AL2. Point of origin of the power to influence or command thought, opinion, or behavior.

权威来源（《权威》第二课）：影响或控制人们的思想、观点或行为的权力的来源

state of nature AL3. An imaginary condition in which people live together without government.

自然状态（《权威》第三课）：一种想象中的状态，人们共同生活在没有政府的环境中。

Supreme Being AL2. God

至高无上的神（《权威》第二课）：上帝。

temperance AL4. Moderation in or abstinence from the use of intoxicating drink.

禁酒（《权威》第四课）：节制或戒除含酒精的饮料。

vigilance AL8. Watchfulness, especially to avoid danger.

警觉（《权威》第八课）：特指为避免危险的警惕性。

welfare program AL5. A system by which the government provides financial aid to needy people.

福利计划（《权威》第五课）：政府为贫困民众提供财政援助的计划。

wildlife preservation AL7. Keeping animals that are not domesticated safe from injury, harm, or destruction.

野生动物保护（《权威》第七课）：保障非驯养动物的安全，使它们免于损伤、危害或毁灭。

woman suffrage AL4. A woman's right to vote.

妇女选举权（《权威》第四课）：妇女投票选举的权利。

writ of habeas corpus AL12. A writ issued to bring a person before a court or judge to obtain protection against illegal imprisonment.

人身保护令（《权威》第十二课）：由法院签发的命令，要求羁押者将被羁押者提交法院或法官（以审查羁押的合法性），以保护个人不受非法拘禁。

附录2：

The Constitution of the United States

We the People of the United States, in[注] Order to form a more perfect Union, establish Justice, insure domestic Tranquility, provide for the common defence, promote the general Welfare, and secure the Blessings of Liberty to ourselves and our Posterity, do ordain and establish this Constitution for the United States of America.

Article. I.

Section. 1   All legislative Powers herein granted shall be vested in a Congress of the United States, which shall consist of a Senate and House of Representatives.

Section. 2   The House of Representatives shall be composed of Members chosen every second Year by the People of the several States, and the Electors in each State shall have the Qualifications requisite for Electors of the most numerous Branch of the State Legislature.

No Person shall be a Representative who shall not have attained to the Age of twenty five Years, and been seven Years a Citizen of the United States, and who shall not, when elected, be an Inhabitant of that State in which he shall be chosen.

Representatives and direct Taxes shall be apportioned among the several States which may be included within this Union, according to their respective Numbers, which shall be determined by adding to the whole Number of free Persons, including those bound to Service for a Term of Years, and excluding Indians not taxed, three fifths of all other Persons. The actual Enumeration shall be made within three Years after the first Meeting of the Congress of the United States, and within every subsequent Term of ten Years, in such Manner as they shall by Law direct. The Number of Representatives shall not exceed one for every thirty Thousand, but each State shall have at Least one Representative; and until

---

注：原文：美国国家档案馆

　　http://www.archives.gov/exhibits/charters/constitution_transcript.html

美利坚合众国宪法

我们合众国人民，为建立更完善的联邦，树立正义，保障国内安宁，提供共同防务，促进公共福利，并使我们自己和后代得享自由的幸福，特为美利坚合众国制定本宪法。

第一条

第一款　本宪法授予的全部立法权，属于由参议院和众议院组成的合众国国会。

第二款　众议院由各州人民每两年选举产生的众议员组成。每个州的选举人须具备该州州议会人数最多一院选举人所必需的资格。

凡年龄不满二十五岁，成为合众国公民不满七年，在一州当选时不是该州居民者，不得担任众议员。

〔众议员名额和直接税税额，在本联邦可包括的各州中，按照各自人口比例进行分配。各州人口数，按自由人总数加上所有其他人口的五分之三予以确定。自由人总数包括必须服一定年限劳役的人，但不包括未被征税的印第安人。〕① 人口的实际统计在合众国国会第一次会议后三年内和此后每十年内，依法律规定的方式进行。每三万人选出的众议员人数不得超过一名，但每州至少须有一名众议员；在进行上述人口统计以前，新罕布什尔州有权选出三名，马萨诸塞州八名，罗得岛州和普罗维登斯种植地一名，康涅狄格州五名，纽约州六名，新泽西州四名，宾夕法尼亚州八名，特拉华州一名，马里兰州六名，弗吉尼亚州十名，北卡罗来纳州五名，南卡罗来纳州五名，佐治亚州三名。

such enumeration shall be made, the State of New Hampshire shall be entitled to chuse three, Massachusetts eight, Rhode-Island and Providence Plantations one, Connecticut five, New-York six, New Jersey four, Pennsylvania eight, Delaware one, Maryland six, Virginia ten, North Carolina five, South Carolina five, and Georgia three.

When vacancies happen in the Representation from any State, the Executive Authority thereof shall issue Writs of Election to fill such Vacancies.

The House of Representatives shall chuse their Speaker and other Officers; and shall have the sole Power of Impeachment.

Section. 3   The Senate of the United States shall be composed of two Senators from each State, chosen by the Legislature thereof for six Years; and each Senator shall have one Vote.

Immediately after they shall be assembled in Consequence of the first Election, they shall be divided as equally as may be into three Classes. The Seats of the Senators of the first Class shall be vacated at the Expiration of the second Year, of the second Class at the Expiration of the fourth Year, and of the third Class at the Expiration of the sixth Year, so that one third may be chosen every second Year; and if Vacancies happen by Resignation, or otherwise, during the Recess of the Legislature of any State, the Executive thereof may make temporary Appointments until the next Meeting of the Legislature, which shall then fill such Vacancies.

No Person shall be a Senator who shall not have attained to the Age of thirty Years, and been nine Years a Citizen of the United States, and who shall not, when elected, be an Inhabitant of that State for which he shall be chosen.

The Vice President of the United States shall be President of the Senate, but shall have no Vote, unless they be equally divided.

The Senate shall chuse their other Officers, and also a President pro tempore, in the Absence of the Vice President, or when he shall exercise the Office of President of the United States.

The Senate shall have the sole Power to try all Impeachments. When sitting for that Purpose, they shall be on Oath or Affirmation. When the President of the United States is tried, the Chief Justice shall preside: And no Person shall be convicted without the Concurrence of two thirds of the Members present.

任何一州代表出现缺额时，该州行政当局应发布选举令，以填补此项缺额。

众议院选举本院议长和其他官员，并独自拥有弹劾权。

第三款　合众国参议院由［每州州议会选举的］②两名参议员组成，任期六年；每名参议员有一票表决权。

参议员在第一次选举后集会时，立即分为人数尽可能相等的三个组。第一组参议员席位在第二年年终空出，第二组参议员席位在第四年年终空出，第三组参议员席位在第六年年终空出，以便三分之一的参议员得每二年改选一次。［在任何一州州议会休会期间，如因辞职或其他原因而出现缺额时，该州行政长官在州议会下次集会填补此项缺额前，得任命临时参议员。］③

凡年龄不满三十岁，成为合众国公民不满九年，在一州当选时不是该州居民者，不得担任参议员。

合众国副总统任参议院议长，但除非参议员投票时赞成票和反对票相等，无表决权。

参议院选举本院其他官员，并在副总统缺席或行使合众国总统职权时，选举一名临时议长。

参议院独自拥有审判一切弹劾案的权力。为此目的而开庭时，全体参议员须宣誓或作代誓宣言。合众国总统受审时，最高法院首席大法官主持审判。无论何人，非经出席参议员三分之二的同意，不得被定罪。

Judgment in Cases of Impeachment shall not extend further than to removal from Office, and disqualification to hold and enjoy any Office of honor, Trust or Profit under the United States: but the Party convicted shall nevertheless be liable and subject to Indictment, Trial, Judgment and Punishment, according to Law.

Section. 4   The Times, Places and Manner of holding Elections for Senators and Representatives, shall be prescribed in each State by the Legislature thereof; but the Congress may at any time by Law make or alter such Regulations, except as to the Places of chusing Senators.

The Congress shall assemble at least once in every Year, and such Meeting shall be on the first Monday in December, unless they shall by Law appoint a different Day.

Section. 5   Each House shall be the Judge of the Elections, Returns and Qualifications of its own Members, and a Majority of each shall constitute a Quorum to do Business; but a smaller Number may adjourn from day to day, and may be authorized to compel the Attendance of absent Members, in such Manner, and under such Penalties as each House may provide.

Each House may determine the Rules of its Proceedings, punish its Members for disorderly Behaviour, and, with the Concurrence of two thirds, expel a Member.

Each House shall keep a Journal of its Proceedings, and from time to time publish the same, excepting such Parts as may in their Judgment require Secrecy; and the Yeas and Nays of the Members of either House on any question shall, at the Desire of one fifth of those Present, be entered on the Journal.

Neither House, during the Session of Congress, shall, without the Consent of the other, adjourn for more than three days, nor to any other Place than that in which the two Houses shall be sitting.

Section. 6   The Senators and Representatives shall receive a Compensation for their Services, to be ascertained by Law, and paid out of the Treasury of the United States. They shall in all Cases, except Treason, Felony and Breach of the Peace, be privileged from Arrest during their Attendance at the Session of their respective Houses, and in going to and returning from the same; and for any Speech or Debate in either House, they shall not be questioned in any other Place.

弹劾案的判决，不得超出免职和剥夺担任和享有合众国属下有荣誉、有责任或有薪金的任何职务的资格。但被定罪的人，仍可依法起诉、审判、判决和惩罚。

第四款　举行参议员和众议员选举的时间、地点和方式，在每个州由该州议会规定。但除选举参议员的地点外，国会得随时以法律制定或改变这类规定。

国会每年至少开会一次，除非国会以法律另订日期外，此会议在［十二月第一个星期一］④举行。

第五款　每院是本院议员的选举、选举结果报告和资格的裁判者。每院议员过半数，即构成议事的法定人数；但不足法定人数时，得逐日休会，并有权按每院规定的方式和罚则，强迫缺席议员出席会议。

每院得规定本院议事规则，惩罚本院议员扰乱秩序的行为，并经三之二议员的同意开除议员。

每院应有本院会议记录，并不时予以公布，但它认为需要保密的部分除外。每院议员对于任何问题的赞成票和反对票，在出席议员五分之一的请求下，应载入会议记录。

在国会开会期间，任何一院，未经另一院同意，不得休会三日以上，也不得到非两院开会的任何地方休会。

第六款　参议员和众议员应得到服务的报酬，此项报酬由法律确定并由合众国国库支付。他们除犯叛国罪、重罪和妨害治安罪外，在一切情况下都享有在出席各自议院会议期间和往返于各自议院途中不受逮捕的特权。他们不得因在各自议院发表的演说或辩论而在任何其他地方受到质问。

No Senator or Representative shall, during the Time for which he was elected, be appointed to any civil Office under the Authority of the United States, which shall have been created, or the Emoluments whereof shall have been encreased during such time; and no Person holding any Office under the United States, shall be a Member of either House during his Continuance in Office.

Section. 7   All Bills for raising Revenue shall originate in the House of Representatives; but the Senate may propose or concur with Amendments as on other Bills.

Every Bill which shall have passed the House of Representatives and the Senate, shall, before it become a Law, be presented to the President of the United States: If he approve he shall sign it, but if not he shall return it, with his Objections to that House in which it shall have originated, who shall enter the Objections at large on their Journal, and proceed to reconsider it. If after such Reconsideration two thirds of that House shall agree to pass the Bill, it shall be sent, together with the Objections, to the other House, by which it shall likewise be reconsidered, and if approved by two thirds of that House, it shall become a Law. But in all such Cases the Votes of both Houses shall be determined by yeas and Nays, and the Names of the Persons voting for and against the Bill shall be entered on the Journal of each House respectively. If any Bill shall not be returned by the President within ten Days (Sundays excepted) after it shall have been presented to him, the Same shall be a Law, in like Manner as if he had signed it, unless the Congress by their Adjournment prevent its Return, in which Case it shall not be a Law.

Every Order, Resolution, or Vote to which the Concurrence of the Senate and House of Representatives may be necessary (except on a question of Adjournment) shall be presented to the President of the United States; and before the Same shall take Effect, shall be approved by him, or being disapproved by him, shall be repassed by two thirds of the Senate and House of Representatives, according to the Rules and Limitations prescribed in the Case of a Bill.

Section. 8   The Congress shall have Power To lay and collect Taxes, Duties, Imposts and Excises, to pay the Debts and provide for the common Defence and general Welfare of the United States; but all Duties, Imposts and Excises shall be uniform throughout the United States;

参议员或众议员在当选任期内，不得被任命担任在此期间设置或增薪的合众国管辖下的任何文官职务。凡在合众国属下任职者，在继续任职期间不得担任任何一院议员。

第七款　所有征税议案应首先在众议院提出，但参议院得像对其他议案一样，提出或同意修正案。

众议院和参议院通过的每一议案，在成为法律前须送交合众国总统。总统如批准该议案，即应签署；如不批准，则应将该议案同其反对意见退回最初提出该议案的议院。该院应特此项反对见详细载入本院会议记录并进行复议。如经复议后，该院三分之二议员同意通过该议案，该议案连同反对意见应一起送交另一议院，并同样由该院进行复议，如经该院三分之二议员赞同，该议案即成为法律。但在所有这类情况下，两院表决都由赞成票和反对票决定；对该议案投赞成票和反对票的议员姓名应分别载入每一议院会议记录。如任何议案在送交总统后十天内（星期日除外）未经总统退回，该议案如同总统已签署一样，即成为法律，除非因国会休会而使该议案不能退回，在此种情况下，该议案不能成为法律。

凡须由参议院和众议院一致同意的每项命令、决议或表决（关于休会问题除外），须送交合众国总统，该项命令、决议或表决在生效前，须由总统批准，如总统不批准，则按照关于议案所规定的规则和限制，由参议院和众议院三分之二议员重新通过。

第八款　国会有权：

规定和征收直接税、进口税、捐税和其他税，以偿付国债、提供合众国共同防务和公共福利，但一切进口税、捐税和其他税应全国统一；

To borrow Money on the credit of the United States;

To regulate Commerce with foreign Nations, and among the several States, and with the Indian Tribes;

To establish an uniform Rule of Naturalization, and uniform Laws on the subject of Bankruptcies throughout the United States;

To coin Money, regulate the Value thereof, and of foreign Coin, and fix the Standard of Weights and Measures;

To provide for the Punishment of counterfeiting the Securities and current Coin of the United States;

To establish Post Offices and post Roads;

To promote the Progress of Science and useful Arts, by securing for limited Times to Authors and Inventors the exclusive Right to their respective Writings and Discoveries;

To constitute Tribunals inferior to the supreme Court;

To define and punish Piracies and Felonies committed on the high Seas, and Offences against the Law of Nations;

To declare War, grant Letters of Marque and Reprisal, and make Rules concerning Captures on Land and Water;

To raise and support Armies, but no Appropriation of Money to that Use shall be for a longer Term than two Years;

To provide and maintain a Navy;

To make Rules for the Government and Regulation of the land and naval Forces;

To provide for calling forth the Militia to execute the Laws of the Union, suppress Insurrections and repel Invasions;

To provide for organizing, arming, and disciplining, the Militia, and for governing such Part of them as may be employed in the Service of the United States, reserving to the States respectively, the Appointment of the Officers, and the Authority of training the Militia according to the discipline prescribed by Congress;

以合众国的信用借款；

管制同外国的、各州之间的和同印第安部落的商业；

制定合众国全国统一的归化条例和破产法；

铸造货币，厘定本国货币和外国货币的价值，并确定度量衡的标准；

规定有关伪造合众国证券和通用货币的罚则；

设立邮政局和修建邮政道路；

保障著作家和发明家对各自著作和发明在限定期限内的专有权利，以促进科学和工艺的进步；

设立低于最高法院的法院；

界定和惩罚在公海上所犯的海盗罪和重罪以及违反国际法的犯罪行为；

宣战，颁发掳获敌船许可状，制定关于陆上和水上捕获的条例；

招募陆军和供给军需，但此项用途的拨款期限不得超过两年；

建立和维持一支海军；

制定治理和管理陆海军的条例；

规定征召民兵，以执行联邦法律、镇压叛乱和击退入侵；

规定民兵的组织、装备和训练，规定用来为合众国服役的那些民兵的管理，但民兵军官的任命和按国会规定的条例训练民兵的权力，由各州保留。

To exercise exclusive Legislation in all Cases whatsoever, over such District (not exceeding ten Miles square) as may, by Cession of particular States, and the Acceptance of Congress, become the Seat of the Government of the United States, and to exercise like Authority over all Places purchased by the Consent of the Legislature of the State in which the Same shall be, for the Erection of Forts, Magazines, Arsenals, dock-Yards, and other needful Buildings;--And To make all Laws which shall be necessary and proper for carrying into Execution the foregoing Powers, and all other Powers vested by this Constitution in the Government of the United States, or in any Department or Officer thereof.

Section. 9　The Migration or Importation of such Persons as any of the States now existing shall think proper to admit, shall not be prohibited by the Congress prior to the Year one thousand eight hundred and eight, but a Tax or duty may be imposed on such Importation, not exceeding ten dollars for each Person.

The Privilege of the Writ of Habeas Corpus shall not be suspended, unless when in Cases of Rebellion or Invasion the public Safety may require it.

No Bill of Attainder or ex post facto Law shall be passed.

No Capitation, or other direct, Tax shall be laid, unless in Proportion to the Census or enumeration herein before directed to be taken.

No Tax or Duty shall be laid on Articles exported from any State.

No Preference shall be given by any Regulation of Commerce or Revenue to the Ports of one State over those of another; nor shall Vessels bound to, or from, one State, be obliged to enter, clear, or pay Duties in another.

No Money shall be drawn from the Treasury, but in Consequence of Appropriations made by Law; and a regular Statement and Account of the Receipts and Expenditures of all public Money shall be published from time to time.

No Title of Nobility shall be granted by the United States: And no Person holding any Office of Profit or Trust under them, shall, without the Consent of the Congress, accept of any present, Emolument, Office, or Title, of any kind whatever, from any King, Prince, or foreign State.

对于由某些州让与合众国、经国会接受而成为合众国政府所在地的地区（不得超过十平方英里），在任何情况下都行使独有的立法权；对于经州议会同意、由合众国在该州购买的用于建造要塞、弹药库、兵工厂、船坞和其他必要建筑物的一切地方，行使同样的权力；以及制定为行使上述各项权力和由本宪法授予合众国政府或其任何部门或官员的一切其他权力所必要和适当的所有法律。

第九款　现有任何一州认为得准予入境之人的迁移或入境，在一千八百零八年以前，国会不得加以禁止，但对此种人的入境，每人可征不超过十美元的税。不得中止人身保护状的特权，除非发生叛乱或入侵时公共安全要求中止这项特权。

不得通过公民权利剥夺法案或追溯既往的法律。

［除依本宪法上文规定的人口普查或统计的比例，不得征收人头税或其他直接税。］⑤

对于从任何一州输出的货物，不得征税。

任何商业或税收条例，都不得给予一州港口以优惠于他州港口的待遇；开往或开出一州的船舶，不得被强迫在他州入港、出港或纳税。

除根据法律规定的拨款外，不得从国库提取款项。一切公款收支的定期报告书和账目，应不时予以公布。

合众国不得授予贵族爵位。凡在合众国属下担任任何有薪金或有责任的职务的人，未经国会同意，不得从任何国王、君主或外国接受任何礼物、俸禄、官职或任何一种爵位。

Section. 10   No State shall enter into any Treaty, Alliance, or Confederation; grant Letters of Marque and Reprisal; coin Money; emit Bills of Credit; make any Thing but gold and silver Coin a Tender in Payment of Debts; pass any Bill of Attainder, ex post facto Law, or Law impairing the Obligation of Contracts, or grant any Title of Nobility.

No State shall, without the Consent of the Congress, lay any Imposts or Duties on Imports or Exports, except what may be absolutely necessary for executing it's inspection Laws: and the net Produce of all Duties and Imposts, laid by any State on Imports or Exports, shall be for the Use of the Treasury of the United States; and all such Laws shall be subject to the Revision and Controul of the Congress.

No State shall, without the Consent of Congress, lay any Duty of Tonnage, keep Troops, or Ships of War in time of Peace, enter into any Agreement or Compact with another State, or with a foreign Power, or engage in War, unless actually invaded, or in such imminent Danger as will not admit of delay.

Article. II.

Section. 1   The executive Power shall be vested in a President of the United States of America. He shall hold his Office during the Term of four Years, and, together with the Vice President, chosen for the same Term, be elected, as follows:

Each State shall appoint, in such Manner as the Legislature thereof may direct, a Number of Electors, equal to the whole Number of Senators and Representatives to which the State may be entitled in the Congress: but no Senator or Representative, or Person holding an Office of Trust or Profit under the United States, shall be appointed an Elector.

The Electors shall meet in their respective States, and vote by Ballot for two Persons, of whom one at least shall not be an Inhabitant of the same State with themselves. And they shall make a List of all the Persons voted for, and of the Number of Votes for each; which List they shall sign and certify, and transmit sealed to the Seat of the Government of the United States, directed to the President of the Senate. The President of the Senate shall, in the Presence of the Senate and House of Representatives, open all the Certificates, and the Votes shall then be counted. The Person

第十款　任何一州都不得：缔结任何条约，参加任何同盟或邦联；颁发捕获敌船许可状；铸造货币；发行纸币；使用金银币以外的任何物品作为偿还债务的货币；通过任何公民权利剥夺法案、追溯既往的法律或损害契约义务的法律；或授予任何贵族爵位。

任何一州，未经国会同意，不得对进口货或出口货征收任何税款，但为执行本州检查法所绝对必需者除外。任何一州对进口货或出口货所征全部税款的纯收益供合众国国库使用；所有这类法律得由国会加以修正和控制。

任何一州，未经国会同意，不得征收任何船舶吨位税，不得在和平时期保持军队或战舰，不得与他州或外国缔结协定或盟约，除非实际遭到入侵或遇刻不容缓的紧迫危险时不得进行战争。

第二条

第一款　行政权属于美利坚合众国总统。总统任期四年，副总统的任期相同。总统和副总统按以下方法选举；每个州依照该州议会所定方式选派选举人若干人，其数目同该州在国会应有的参议员和众议员总人数相等。但参议员或众议员，或在合众国属下担任有责任或有薪金职务的人，不得被选派为选举人。

［选举人在各自州内集会，投票选举两人，其中至少有一人不是选举人本州的居民。选举人须开列名单，写明所有被选人和每人所得票数；在该名单上签名作证，将封印后的名单送合众国政府所在地，交参议院议长收。参议院议长在参议院和众议院全体议员面前开拆所有证明书，然后计算票数。得票最多的人，如所得票数超过所选派选举人总数的半数，即为总统。如获得此种过半数票的人不止一人，且得票相等，众议院应立即投票选举其中一人为总统。如无人获得过半数票；该院应以同样方式从名单上得票最多的五人中选举一人为总统。但选举总统时，以州为单位计票，每州代表有一票表决权；三分之二的州各有一名或多名众议员出席，即构成选举总统的法定人数，选出总统需要所有州的过半数票。

having the greatest Number of Votes shall be the President, if such Number be a Majority of the whole Number of Electors appointed; and if there be more than one who have such Majority, and have an equal Number of Votes, then the House of Representatives shall immediately chuse by Ballot one of them for President; and if no Person have a Majority, then from the five highest on the List the said House shall in like Manner chuse the President. But in chusing the President, the Votes shall be taken by States, the Representation from each State having one Vote; A quorum for this purpose shall consist of a Member or Members from two thirds of the States, and a Majority of all the States shall be necessary to a Choice. In every Case, after the Choice of the President, the Person having the greatest Number of Votes of the Electors shall be the Vice President. But if there should remain two or more who have equal Votes, the Senate shall chuse from them by Ballot the Vice President.

The Congress may determine the Time of chusing the Electors, and the Day on which they shall give their Votes; which Day shall be the same throughout the United States.

No Person except a natural born Citizen, or a Citizen of the United States, at the time of the Adoption of this Constitution, shall be eligible to the Office of President; neither shall any Person be eligible to that Office who shall not have attained to the Age of thirty five Years, and been fourteen Years a Resident within the United States.

In Case of the Removal of the President from Office, or of his Death, Resignation, or Inability to discharge the Powers and Duties of the said Office, the Same shall devolve on the Vice President, and the Congress may by Law provide for the Case of Removal, Death, Resignation or Inability, both of the President and Vice President, declaring what Officer shall then act as President, and such Officer shall act accordingly, until the Disability be removed, or a President shall be elected.

The President shall, at stated Times, receive for his Services, a Compensation, which shall neither be increased nor diminished during the Period for which he shall have been elected, and he shall not receive within that Period any other Emolument from the United States, or any of them.

在每种情况下，总统选出后，得选举人票最多的人，即为副总统。但如果有两人或两人以上得票相等，参议院应投票选举其中一人为副总统。]⑥

国会得确定选出选举人的时间和选举人投票日期，该日期在全合众国应为同一天。

无论何人，除生为合众国公民或在本宪法采用时已是合众国公民者外，不得当选为总统；凡年龄不满三十五岁、在合众国境内居住不满十四年者，也不得当选为总统。

[如遇总统被免职、死亡、辞职或丧失履行总统权力和责任的能力时，总统职务应移交副总统。国会得以法律规定在总统和副总统两人被免职、死亡、辞职或丧失任职能力时，宣布应代理总统的官员。该官员应代理总统直到总统恢复任职能力或新总统选出为止。]⑦

总统在规定的时间，应得到服务报酬，此项报酬在其当选担任总统任期内不得增加或减少。总统在任期内不得接受合众国或任何一州的任何其他俸禄。

Before he enter on the Execution of his Office, he shall take the following Oath or Affirmation:--"I do solemnly swear (or affirm) that I will faithfully execute the Office of President of the United States, and will to the best of my Ability, preserve, protect and defend the Constitution of the United States."

Section. 2   The President shall be Commander in Chief of the Army and Navy of the United States, and of the Militia of the several States, when called into the actual Service of the United States; he may require the Opinion, in writing, of the principal Officer in each of the executive Departments, upon any Subject relating to the Duties of their respective Offices, and he shall have Power to grant Reprieves and Pardons for Offences against the United States, except in Cases of Impeachment.

He shall have Power, by and with the Advice and Consent of the Senate, to make Treaties, provided two thirds of the Senators present concur; and he shall nominate, and by and with the Advice and Consent of the Senate, shall appoint Ambassadors, other public Ministers and Consuls, Judges of the supreme Court, and all other Officers of the United States, whose Appointments are not herein otherwise provided for, and which shall be established by Law: but the Congress may by Law vest the Appointment of such inferior Officers, as they think proper, in the President alone, in the Courts of Law, or in the Heads of Departments.

The President shall have Power to fill up all Vacancies that may happen during the Recess of the Senate, by granting Commissions which shall expire at the End of their next Session.

Section. 3   He shall from time to time give to the Congress Information of the State of the Union, and recommend to their Consideration such Measures as he shall judge necessary and expedient; he may, on extraordinary Occasions, convene both Houses, or either of them, and in Case of Disagreement between them, with Respect to the Time of Adjournment, he may adjourn them to such Time as he shall think proper; he shall receive Ambassadors and other public Ministers; he shall take Care that the Laws be faithfully executed, and shall Commission all the Officers of the United States.

Section. 4   The President, Vice President and all civil Officers of the United States, shall be removed from Office on Impeachment for, and Conviction of, Treason, Bribery, or other high Crimes and Misdemeanors.

总统在开始执行职务前，应作如下宣誓或代誓宣言："我庄严宣誓（或宣言）我一定忠实执行合众国总统职务，竭尽全力维护、保护和捍卫合众国宪法"。

第二款　总统是合众国陆军、海军和征调为合众国服役的各州民兵的总司令。他得要求每个行政部门长官就他们各自职责有关的任何事项提出书面意见。他有权对危害合众国的犯罪行为发布缓刑令和赦免令，但弹劾案除外。

总统经咨询参议院和取得其同意有权缔结条约，但须经出席参议员三分之二的批准。他提名，并经咨询参议院和取得其同意，任命大使、公使和领事、最高法院法官和任命手续未由本宪法另行规定而应由法律规定的合众国所有其他官员。但国会认为适当时，得以法律将这类低级官员的任命权授予总统一人、法院或各部部长。

总统有权委任人员填补在参议院休会期间可能出现的官员缺额，此项委任在参议院下期会议结束时满期。

第三款　总统应不时向国会报告联邦情况，并向国会提出他认为必要和妥善的措施供国会审议。在非常情况下，他得召集两院或任何一院开会。如遇两院对休会时间有意见分歧时，他可使两院休会到他认为适当的时间。他应接见大使和公使。他应负责使法律切实执行，并委任合众国的所有官员。

第四款　总统、副总统和合众国的所有文职官员，因叛国、贿赂或其他重罪和轻罪而受弹劾并被定罪时，应予免职。

Article III.

Section. 1   The judicial Power of the United States shall be vested in one supreme Court, and in such inferior Courts as the Congress may from time to time ordain and establish. The Judges, both of the supreme and inferior Courts, shall hold their Offices during good Behaviour, and shall, at stated Times, receive for their Services a Compensation, which shall not be diminished during their Continuance in Office.

Section. 2   The judicial Power shall extend to all Cases, in Law and Equity, arising under this Constitution, the Laws of the United States, and Treaties made, or which shall be made, under their Authority;--to all Cases affecting Ambassadors, other public Ministers and Consuls;--to all Cases of admiralty and maritime Jurisdiction;--to Controversies to which the United States shall be a Party;--to Controversies between two or more States;-- between a State and Citizens of another State,--between Citizens of different States,--between Citizens of the same State claiming Lands under Grants of different States, and between a State, or the Citizens thereof, and foreign States, Citizens or Subjects.

In all Cases affecting Ambassadors, other public Ministers and Consuls, and those in which a State shall be Party, the supreme Court shall have original Jurisdiction. In all the other Cases before mentioned, the supreme Court shall have appellate Jurisdiction, both as to Law and Fact, with such Exceptions, and under such Regulations as the Congress shall make.

The Trial of all Crimes, except in Cases of Impeachment, shall be by Jury; and such Trial shall be held in the State where the said Crimes shall have been committed; but when not committed within any State, the Trial shall be at such Place or Places as the Congress may by Law have directed.

Section. 3   Treason against the United States, shall consist only in levying War against them, or in adhering to their Enemies, giving them Aid and Comfort. No Person shall be convicted of Treason unless on the Testimony of two Witnesses to the same overt Act, or on Confession in open Court.

The Congress shall have Power to declare the Punishment of Treason, but no Attainder of Treason shall work Corruption of Blood, or Forfeiture except during the Life of the Person attainted.

第三条

第一款　合众国的司法权，属于最高法院和国会不时规定和设立的下级法院。最高法院和下级法院的法官如行为端正，得继续任职，并应在规定的时间得到服务报酬，此项报酬在他们继续任职期间不得减少。

第二款　司法权的适用范围包括：由于本宪法、合众国法律和根据合众国权力已缔结或将缔结的条约而产生的一切普通法的和衡平法的案件；涉及大使、公使和领事的一切案件；关于海事法和海事管辖权的一切案件；合众国为一方当事人的诉讼；两个或两个以上州之间的诉讼；〔一州和他州公民之间的诉讼；〕⑧不同州公民之间的诉讼；同州公民之间对不同州让与土地的所有权的诉讼；一州或其公民同外国或外国公民或国民之间的诉讼。

涉及大使、公使和领事以及一州为一方当事人的一切案件，最高法院具有第一审管辖权。对上述所有其他案件，不论法律方面还是事实方面，最高法院具有上诉审管辖权，但须依照国会所规定的例外和规章。

除弹劾案外，一切犯罪由陪审团审判；此种审判应在犯罪发生的州内举行；但如犯罪不发生在任何一州之内，审判应在国会以法律规定的一个或几个地点举行。

第三款　对合众国的叛国罪只限于同合众国作战，或依附其敌人，给予其敌人以帮助和鼓励。无论何人，除根据两个证人对同一明显行为的作证或本人在公开法庭上的供认，不得被定为叛国罪。

国会有权宣告对叛国罪的惩罚，但因叛国罪而剥夺公民权，不得造成血统玷污，除非在被剥夺者在世期间，也不得没收其财产。

Article. IV.

Section. 1   Full Faith and Credit shall be given in each State to the public Acts, Records, and judicial Proceedings of every other State. And the Congress may by general Laws prescribe the Manner in which such Acts, Records and Proceedings shall be proved, and the Effect thereof.

Section. 2   The Citizens of each State shall be entitled to all Privileges and Immunities of Citizens in the several States.

A Person charged in any State with Treason, Felony, or other Crime, who shall flee from Justice, and be found in another State, shall on Demand of the executive Authority of the State from which he fled, be delivered up, to be removed to the State having Jurisdiction of the Crime.

No Person held to Service or Labour in one State, under the Laws thereof, escaping into another, shall, in Consequence of any Law or Regulation therein, be discharged from such Service or Labour, but shall be delivered up on Claim of the Party to whom such Service or Labour may be due.

Section. 3   New States may be admitted by the Congress into this Union; but no new State shall be formed or erected within the Jurisdiction of any other State; nor any State be formed by the Junction of two or more States, or Parts of States, without the Consent of the Legislatures of the States concerned as well as of the Congress.

The Congress shall have Power to dispose of and make all needful Rules and Regulations respecting the Territory or other Property belonging to the United States; and nothing in this Constitution shall be so construed as to Prejudice any Claims of the United States, or of any particular State.

Section. 4   The United States shall guarantee to every State in this Union a Republican Form of Government, and shall protect each of them against Invasion; and on Application of the Legislature, or of the Executive (when the Legislature cannot be convened), against domestic Violence.

第四条

第一款　每个州对于他州的公共法律、案卷和司法程序，应给予充分信任和尊重。国会得以一般法律规定这类法律、案卷和司法程序如何证明和具有的效力。

第二款　每个州的公民享有各州公民的一切特权和豁免权。

在任何一州被控告犯有叛国罪、重罪或其他罪行的人，逃脱法网而在他州被寻获时，应根据他所逃出之州行政当局的要求将他交出，以便解送到对犯罪行为有管辖权的州。

［根据一州法律须在该州服劳役或劳动的人，如逃往他州，不得因他州的法律或规章而免除此种劳役或劳动，而应根据有权得到此劳役或劳动之当事人的要求将他交出。］⑨

第三款　新州得由国会接纳加入本联邦；但不得在任何其他州的管辖范围内组成或建立新州；未经有关州议会和国会的同意，也不得合并两个或两个以上的州或几个州的一部分组成新州。

国会对于属于合众国的领土或其他财产，有权处置和制定一切必要的条例和规章。对本宪法条文不得作有损于合众国或任何一州的任何权利的解释。

第四款　合众国保证本联邦各州实行共和政体，保护每州免遭入侵，并应州议会或州行政长官（在州议会不能召开时）的请求平定内乱。

Article. V.

The Congress, whenever two thirds of both Houses shall deem it necessary, shall propose Amendments to this Constitution, or, on the Application of the Legislatures of two thirds of the several States, shall call a Convention for proposing Amendments, which, in either Case, shall be valid to all Intents and Purposes, as Part of this Constitution, when ratified by the Legislatures of three fourths of the several States, or by Conventions in three fourths thereof, as the one or the other Mode of Ratification may be proposed by the Congress; Provided that no Amendment which may be made prior to the Year One thousand eight hundred and eight shall in any Manner affect the first and fourth Clauses in the Ninth Section of the first Article; and that no State, without its Consent, shall be deprived of its equal Suffrage in the Senate.

Article. VI.

All Debts contracted and Engagements entered into, before the Adoption of this Constitution, shall be as valid against the United States under this Constitution, as under the Confederation.

This Constitution, and the Laws of the United States which shall be made in Pursuance thereof; and all Treaties made, or which shall be made, under the Authority of the United States, shall be the supreme Law of the Land; and the Judges in every State shall be bound thereby, any Thing in the Constitution or Laws of any State to the Contrary notwithstanding.

The Senators and Representatives before mentioned, and the Members of the several State Legislatures, and all executive and judicial Officers, both of the United States and of the several States, shall be bound by Oath or Affirmation, to support this Constitution; but no religious Test shall ever be required as a Qualification to any Office or public Trust under the United States.

Article. VII.

The Ratification of the Conventions of nine States, shall be sufficient for the Establishment of this Constitution between the States so ratifying the Same.

第五条

国会在两院三分之二议员认为必要时，应提出本宪法的修正案，或根据各州三分之二州议会的请求，召开制宪会议提出修正案。不论哪种方式提出的修正案，经各州四分之三州议会或四分之三州制宪会议的批准，即实际成为本宪法的一部分而发生效力；采用哪种批准方式，得由国会提出建议。但［在一千八百零八年以前制定的修正案，不得以任何形式影响本宪法第一条第九款第一项和第四项］；⑩任何一州，不经其同意，不得被剥夺它在参议院的平等投票权。

第六条

本宪法采用前订立的一切债务和承担的一切义务，对于实行本宪法的合众国同邦联时期一样有效。

本宪法和依本宪法所制定的合众国法律，以及根据合众国的权力已缔结或将缔结的一切条约，都是全国的最高法律；每个州的法官都应受其约束，即使州的宪法和法律中有与之相抵触的内容。

上述参议员和众议员，各州州议会议员，以及合众国和各州所有行政和司法官员，应宣誓或作代誓宣言拥护本宪法；但决不得以宗教信仰作为担任合众国属下任何官职或公职的必要资格。

第七条

经九个州制宪会议的批准，即足以使本宪法在各批准州成立。

Done in Convention by the Unanimous Consent of the States present the Seventeenth Day of September in the Year of our Lord one thousand seven hundred and Eighty seven and of the Independance of the United States of America the Twelfth In witness whereof We have hereunto subscribed our Names.

G°. Washington

Presidt and deputy from Virginia

Delaware

Geo: Read   Gunning Bedford jun

John Dickinson   Richard Bassett

Jaco: Broom

Maryland

James McHenry   Dan of St Thos. Jenifer

Danl. Carroll

Virginia

John Blair   James Madison Jr.

North Carolina

Wm. Blount   Richd. Dobbs Spaight

Hu Williamson

South Carolina

J. Rutledge   Charles Cotesworth Pinckney

Charles Pinckney   Pierce Butler

Georgia

William Few   Abr Baldwin

New Hampshire

John Langdon   Nicholas Gilman

本宪法于耶稣纪元一千七百八十七年，即美利坚合众国独立后第十二年的九月十七日，经出席各州在制宪会议上一致同意后制定。我们谨在此签名作证。

乔治·华盛顿
主席、弗吉尼亚州代表
特拉华州

乔治·里德　　　　　　　　小冈宁·贝德福德

约翰·迪金森　　　　　　　理查德·巴西特

雅各布·布鲁姆

马里兰州

詹姆斯·麦克亨利　　　　　圣托马斯·詹尼弗的丹尼尔

丹尼尔·卡罗尔

弗吉尼亚州

约翰·布莱尔　　　　　　　小詹姆斯·麦迪逊

北卡罗来纳州

威廉·布朗特　　　　　　　理查德·多布斯·斯佩特

休·威廉森

南卡罗来纳州

约翰·拉特利奇　　　　　　查尔斯·科茨沃斯·平克尼

查尔斯·平克尼　　　　　　皮尔斯·巴特勒

佐治亚州

威廉·费尤　　　　　　　　亚伯拉罕·鲍德温

新罕布什尔州

约翰·兰登　　　　　　　　尼古拉斯·吉尔曼

Massachusetts

Nathaniel Gorham   Rufus King

Connecticut

Wm. Saml. Johnson   Roger Sherman

New York

Alexander Hamilton

New Jersey

Wil: Livingston   David Brearley

Wm. Paterson   Jona: Dayton

Pennsylvania

B Franklin   Thomas Mifflin

Robt. Morris   Geo. Clymer

Thos. FitzSimons   Jared Ingersoll

James Wilson   Gouv Morris

Attest William Jackson Secretary

The Bill of Rights:

Amendment I

Congress shall make no law respecting an establishment of religion, or prohibiting the free exercise thereof; or abridging the freedom of speech, or of the press; or the right of the people peaceably to assemble, and to petition the Government for a redress of grievances.

马萨诸塞州

纳撒尼尔·戈勒姆　　　　　　鲁弗斯·金

康涅狄格州

威廉·塞缪尔·约翰逊　　　　罗杰·谢尔曼

纽约州

亚历山大·汉密尔顿

新泽西州

威廉·利文斯顿　　　　　　　戴维·布里尔利

威廉·帕特森　　　　　　　　乔纳森·戴顿

宾夕法尼亚州

本杰明·富兰克林　　　　　　托马斯·米夫林

罗伯特·莫里斯　　　　　　　乔治·克莱默

托马斯·菲茨西蒙斯　　　　　贾雷德·英格索尔

詹姆斯·威尔逊　　　　　　　古·莫里斯

证人：威廉·杰克逊，秘书

《权利法案》：

（依照原宪法第五条、由国会提出并经各州批准、增添和修改美利坚合众国宪法的条款。译者注）

第一条修正案

［前十条修正案于 1789 年 9 月 25 日提出，1791 年 12 月 15 日批准，被称为"权利法案"。］

国会不得制定关于下列事项的法律：确立国教或禁止信教自由；剥夺言论自由或出版自由；或剥夺人民和平集会和向政府请愿伸冤的权利。

Amendment II

A well regulated Militia, being necessary to the security of a free State, the right of the people to keep and bear Arms, shall not be infringed.

Amendment III

No Soldier shall, in time of peace be quartered in any house, without the consent of the Owner, nor in time of war, but in a manner to be prescribed by law.

Amendment IV

The right of the people to be secure in their persons, houses, papers, and effects, against unreasonable searches and seizures, shall not be violated, and no Warrants shall issue, but upon probable cause, supported by Oath or affirmation, and particularly describing the place to be searched, and the persons or things to be seized.

Amendment V

No person shall be held to answer for a capital, or otherwise infamous crime, unless on a presentment or indictment of a Grand Jury, except in cases arising in the land or naval forces, or in the Militia, when in actual service in time of War or public danger; nor shall any person be subject for the same offence to be twice put in jeopardy of life or limb; nor shall be compelled in any criminal case to be a witness against himself, nor be deprived of life, liberty, or property, without due process of law; nor shall private property be taken for public use, without just compensation.

Amendment VI

In all criminal prosecutions, the accused shall enjoy the right to a speedy and public trial, by an impartial jury of the State and district wherein the crime shall have been committed, which district shall have been previously ascertained by law, and to be informed of the nature and cause of the accusation; to be confronted with the witnesses against him; to have compulsory process for obtaining witnesses in his favor, and to have the Assistance of Counsel for his defence.

第二条修正案

管理良好的民兵是保障自由州的安全所必需的，因此人民持有和携带武器的权利不得侵犯。

第三条修正案

未经房主同意，士兵平时不得驻扎在任何住宅；除依法律规定的方式，战时也不得驻扎。

第四条修正案

人民的人身、住宅、文件和财产不受无理搜查和扣押的权利，不得侵犯。除依据可能成立的理由，以宣誓或代誓宣言保证，并详细说明搜查地点和扣押的人或物，不得发出搜查和扣押状。

第五条修正案

无论何人，除非根据大陪审团的报告或起诉书，不受死罪或其他重罪的审判，但发生在陆、海军中或发生在战时或出现公共危险时服役的民兵中的案件除外。任何人不得因同一犯罪行为而两次遭受生命或身体的危害；不得在任何刑事案件中被迫自证其罪；不经正当法律程序，不得被剥夺生命、自由或财产。不给予公平赔偿，私有财产不得充作公用。

第六条修正案

在一切刑事诉讼中，被告有权由犯罪行为发生地的州和地区的公正陪审团予以迅速和公开的审判，该地区应事先已由法律确定；得知控告的性质和理由；同原告证人对质；以强制程序取得对其有利的证人；取得律师帮助为其辩护。

Amendment VII

In Suits at common law, where the value in controversy shall exceed twenty dollars, the right of trial by jury shall be preserved, and no fact tried by a jury, shall be otherwise re-examined in any Court of the United States, than according to the rules of the common law.

Amendment VIII

Excessive bail shall not be required, nor excessive fines imposed, nor cruel and unusual punishments inflicted.

Amendment IX

The enumeration in the Constitution, of certain rights, shall not be construed to deny or disparage others retained by the people.

Amendment X

The powers not delegated to the United States by the Constitution, nor prohibited by it to the States, are reserved to the States respectively, or to the people.

The Constitution: Amendments 11-27

AMENDMENT XI

Passed by Congress March 4, 1794. Ratified February 7, 1795.

Note: Article III, section 2, of the Constitution was modified by amendment 11.

The Judicial power of the United States shall not be construed to extend to any suit in law or equity, commenced or prosecuted against one of the United States by Citizens of another State, or by Citizens or Subjects of any Foreign State.

第七条修正案

在习惯法的诉讼中，其争执价额超过二十美元，由陪审团审判的权利应受到保护。由陪审团裁决的事实，合众国的任何法院除非按照习惯法规则，不得重新审查。

第八条修正案

不得要求过多的保释金，不得处以过重的罚金，不得施加残酷和非常的惩罚。

第九条修正案

本宪法对某些权利的列举，不得被解释为否定或轻视由人民保留的其他权利。

第十条修正案

宪法未授予合众国、也未禁止各州行使的权力，由各州各自保留，或由人民保留。

第十一条修正案

［1794 年 3 月 4 日提出，1795 年 2 月 7 日批准］

合众国的司法权，不得被解释为适用于由他州公民或任何外国公民或国民对合众国一州提出的或起诉的任何普通法或衡平法的诉讼。

AMENDMENT XII

Passed by Congress December 9, 1803. Ratified June 15, 1804.

Note: A portion of Article II, section 1 of the Constitution was superseded by the 12th amendment.

The Electors shall meet in their respective states and vote by ballot for President and Vice-President, one of whom, at least, shall not be an inhabitant of the same state with themselves; they shall name in their ballots the person voted for as President, and in distinct ballots the person voted for as Vice-President, and they shall make distinct lists of all persons voted for as President, and of all persons voted for as Vice-President, and of the number of votes for each, which lists they shall sign and certify, and transmit sealed to the seat of the government of the United States, directed to the President of the Senate; -- the President of the Senate shall, in the presence of the Senate and House of Representatives, open all the certificates and the votes shall then be counted; -- The person having the greatest number of votes for President, shall be the President, if such number be a majority of the whole number of Electors appointed; and if no person have such majority, then from the persons having the highest numbers not exceeding three on the list of those voted for as President, the House of Representatives shall choose immediately, by ballot, the President. But in choosing the President, the votes shall be taken by states, the representation from each state having one vote; a quorum for this purpose shall consist of a member or members from two-thirds of the states, and a majority of all the states shall be necessary to a choice. [And if the House of Representatives shall not choose a President whenever the right of choice shall devolve upon them, before the fourth day of March next following, then the Vice-President shall act as President, as in case of the death or other constitutional disability of the President. --]* The person having the greatest number of votes as Vice-President, shall be the Vice-President, if such number be a majority of the whole number of Electors appointed, and if no person have a majority, then from the two highest numbers on the list, the Senate shall choose the Vice-President; a quorum for the purpose shall consist of two-thirds of the whole number of Senators, and a majority of the whole number shall be necessary to a choice. But no person constitutionally ineligible to the office of President shall be eligible to that of Vice-President of the United States.

第十二条修正案

［1803 年 12 月 9 日提出，1804 年 7 月 27 日批准］

选举人在各自州内集会，投票选举总统和副总统，其中至少有一人不是选举人本州的居民。选举人须在选票上写明被选为总统之人的姓名，并在另一选票上写明校选为副总统之人的姓名。选举人须将所有被选为总统之人和所有被选为副总统之人分别开列名单，写明每人所得票数；在该名单上签名作证，将封印后的名单送合众国政府所在地，交参议院议长收。参议院议长在参议院和众议院全体议员面前开拆所有证明书，然后计算票数。获得总统选票最多的人，如所得票数超过所选派选举人总数的半数，即为总统。如无人获得这种过半数票，众议院应立即从被选为总统之人名单中得票最多的但不超过三人中间，投票选举总统。但选举总统时，以州为单位计票，每州代表有一票表决权。三分之二的州各有一名或多名众议员出席，即构成选举总统的法定人数，选出总统需要所有州的过半数票。［当选举总统的权力转移到众议院时，如该院在次年三月四日前尚未选出总统，则由副总统代理总统，如同总统死亡或宪法规定的其他丧失任职能力的情况一样。］(11)得副总统选票最多的人，如所得票数超过所选派选举人总数的半数，即为副总统。如无人得过半数票，参议院应从名单上得票最多的两人中选举副总统。选举副总统的法定人数由参议员总数的三分之二构成，选出副总统需要参议员总数的过半数票。但依宪法无资格担任总统的人，也无资格担任合众国副总统。

*Superseded by section 3 of the 20th amendment.

AMENDMENT XIII

Passed by Congress January 31, 1865. Ratified December 6, 1865.

Note: A portion of Article IV, section 2, of the Constitution was superseded by the 13th amendment.

Section 1   Neither slavery nor involuntary servitude, except as a punishment for crime whereof the party shall have been duly convicted, shall exist within the United States, or any place subject to their jurisdiction.

Section 2   Congress shall have power to enforce this article by appropriate legislation.

AMENDMENT XIV

Passed by Congress June 13, 1866. Ratified July 9, 1868.

Note: Article I, section 2, of the Constitution was modified by section 2 of the 14th amendment.

Section 1   All persons born or naturalized in the United States, and subject to the jurisdiction thereof, are citizens of the United States and of the State wherein they reside. No State shall make or enforce any law which shall abridge the privileges or immunities of citizens of the United States; nor shall any State deprive any person of life, liberty, or property, without due process of law; nor deny to any person within its jurisdiction the equal protection of the laws.

Section 2   Representatives shall be apportioned among the several States according to their respective numbers, counting the whole number of persons in each State, excluding Indians not taxed. But when the right to vote at any election for the choice of electors for President and Vice-President of the United States, Representatives in Congress, the Executive and Judicial officers of a State, or the members of the Legislature thereof, is denied to any of the male inhabitants of such State, being twenty-one years of age,* and citizens of the United States, or in any way abridged, except for participation in rebellion, or other crime, the basis of representation therein shall be reduced in the proportion which the number of such male citizens shall bear to the whole number of male citizens twenty-one years of age in such State.

第十三条修正案

［1865 年 1 月 31 日提出，1865 年 12 月 6 日批准］

第一款　在合众国境内受合众国管辖的任何地方，奴隶制和强制劳役都不得存在，但作为对于依法判罪的人的犯罪的惩罚除

第二款　国会有权以适当立法实施本条。

第十四条修正案

［1866 年 6 月 13 日提出，1868 年 7 月 9 日批准］

第一款　所有在合众国出生或归化合众国并受其管辖的人，都是合众国的和他们居住州的公民。任何一州，都不得制定或实施限制合众国公民的特权或豁免权的任何法律；不经正当法律程序，不得剥夺任何人的生命、自由或财产；在州管辖范围内，也不得拒绝给予任何人以平等法律保护。

第二款　众议员名额，应按各州人口比例进行分配，此人口数包括一州的全部人口数，但不包括未被征税的印第安人。但在选举合众国总统和副总统选举人、国会众议员、州行政和司法官员或州议会议员的任何选举中，一州的［年满二十一岁］② 并且是合众国公民的任何男性居民，除因参加叛乱或其他犯罪外，如其选举权道到拒绝或受到任何方式的限制，则该州代表权的基础，应按以上男性公民的人数同该州年满二十一岁男性公民总人数的比例予以削减。

Section 3   No person shall be a Senator or Representative in Congress, or elector of President and Vice-President, or hold any office, civil or military, under the United States, or under any State, who, having previously taken an oath, as a member of Congress, or as an officer of the United States, or as a member of any State legislature, or as an executive or judicial officer of any State, to support the Constitution of the United States, shall have engaged in insurrection or rebellion against the same, or given aid or comfort to the enemies thereof. But Congress may by a vote of two-thirds of each House, remove such disability.

Section 4   The validity of the public debt of the United States, authorized by law, including debts incurred for payment of pensions and bounties for services in suppressing insurrection or rebellion, shall not be questioned. But neither the United States nor any State shall assume or pay any debt or obligation incurred in aid of insurrection or rebellion against the United States, or any claim for the loss or emancipation of any slave; but all such debts, obligations and claims shall be held illegal and void.

Section 5   The Congress shall have the power to enforce, by appropriate legislation, the provisions of this article.

*Changed by section 1 of the 26th amendment.

AMENDMENT XV

Passed by Congress February 26, 1869. Ratified February 3, 1870.

Section 1   The right of citizens of the United States to vote shall not be denied or abridged by the United States or by any State on account of race, color, or previous condition of servitude--

Section 2   The Congress shall have the power to enforce this article by appropriate legislation.

AMENDMENT XVI

Passed by Congress July 2, 1909. Ratified February 3, 1913.

Note: Article I, section 9, of the Constitution was modified by amendment 16.

第三款　无论何人，凡先前曾以国会议员、或合众国官员、或任何州议会议员、或任何州行政或司法官员的身份宣誓维护合众国宪法，以后又对合众国作乱或反叛，或给予合众国敌人帮助或鼓励，都不得担任国会参议员或众议员、或总统和副总统选举人，或担任合众国或任何州属下的任何文职或军职官员。但国会得以两院各三分之二的票数取消此种限制。

第四款　对于法律批准的合众国公共债务，包括因支付平定作乱或反叛有功人员的年金和奖金而产生的债务，其效力不得有所怀疑。但无论合众国或任何一州，都不得承担或偿付因援助对合众国的作乱或反叛而产生的任何债务或义务，或因丧失或解放任何奴隶而提出的任何赔偿要求；所有这类债务、义务和要求，都应被认为是非法和无效的。

第五款　国会有权以适当立法实施本条规定。

第十五条修正案
［1869 年 2 月 26 日提出，1870 年 2 月 3 日批准］

第一款　合众国公民的选举权，不得因种族、肤色或以前是奴隶而被合众国或任何一州加以拒绝或限制。

第二款　国会有权以适当立法实施本条。

第十六条修正案
［1909 年 7 月 12 日提出，1913 年 2 月 3 日批准］

The Congress shall have power to lay and collect taxes on incomes, from whatever source derived, without apportionment among the several States, and without regard to any census or enumeration.

AMENDMENT XVII

Passed by Congress May 13, 1912. Ratified April 8, 1913.

Note: Article I, section 3, of the Constitution was modified by the 17th amendment.

The Senate of the United States shall be composed of two Senators from each State, elected by the people thereof, for six years; and each Senator shall have one vote. The electors in each State shall have the qualifications requisite for electors of the most numerous branch of the State legislatures.

When vacancies happen in the representation of any State in the Senate, the executive authority of such State shall issue writs of election to fill such vacancies: Provided, That the legislature of any State may empower the executive thereof to make temporary appointments until the people fill the vacancies by election as the legislature may direct.

This amendment shall not be so construed as to affect the election or term of any Senator chosen before it becomes valid as part of the Constitution.

AMENDMENT XVIII

Passed by Congress December 18, 1917. Ratified January 16, 1919. Repealed by amendment 21.

Section 1   After one year from the ratification of this article the manufacture, sale, or transportation of intoxicating liquors within, the importation thereof into, or the exportation thereof from the United States and all territory subject to the jurisdiction thereof for beverage purposes is hereby prohibited.

Section 2   The Congress and the several States shall have concurrent power to enforce this article by appropriate legislation.

Section 3   This article shall be inoperative unless it shall have been ratified as an amendment to the Constitution by the legislatures of the several States, as provided in the Constitution, within seven years from the date of the submission hereof to the States by the Congress.

国会有权对任何来源的收入规定和征收所得税，无须在各州按比例进行分配，也无须考虑任何人口普查或人口统计。

第十七条修正案

［1912 年 5 月 13 日提出，1913 年 4 月 8 日批准］

合众国参议院由每州人民选举的两名参议员组成，任期六年；每名参议员有一票表决权。每个州的选举人应具备该州州议会人数最多一院选举人所必需的资格。

任何一州在参议院的代表出现缺额时，该州行政当局应发布选举令，以填补此项缺额。但任何一州的议会，在人民依该议会指示举行选举填补缺额以前，得授权本州行政长官任命临时参议员。

本条修正案不得作如此解释，以致影响在本条修正案作为宪法的一部分生效以前当选的任何参议员的选举或任期。

第十八条修正案

［1917 年 12 月 18 日提出，1919 年 1 月 16 日批准］

［第一款　本条批准一年后，禁止在合众国及其管辖下的一切领土内酿造、出售和运送作为饮料的致醉酒类；禁止此类酒类输入或输出合众国及其管辖下的一切领土。

第二款　国会和各州都有权以适当立法实施本条。

第三款　本条除非在国会将其提交各州之日起七年以内，由各州议会按本宪法规定批准为宪法修正案，不得发生效力。］⑬

AMENDMENT XIX

Passed by Congress June 4, 1919. Ratified August 18, 1920.

The right of citizens of the United States to vote shall not be denied or abridged by the United States or by any State on account of sex.

Congress shall have power to enforce this article by appropriate legislation.

AMENDMENT XX

Passed by Congress March 2, 1932. Ratified January 23, 1933.

Note: Article I, section 4, of the Constitution was modified by section 2 of this amendment. In addition, a portion of the 12th amendment was superseded by section 3.

Section 1   The terms of the President and the Vice President shall end at noon on the 20th day of January, and the terms of Senators and Representatives at noon on the 3d day of January, of the years in which such terms would have ended if this article had not been ratified; and the terms of their successors shall then begin.

Section 2   The Congress shall assemble at least once in every year, and such meeting shall begin at noon on the 3d day of January, unless they shall by law appoint a different day.

Section 3   If, at the time fixed for the beginning of the term of the President, the President elect shall have died, the Vice President elect shall become President. If a President shall not have been chosen before the time fixed for the beginning of his term, or if the President elect shall have failed to qualify, then the Vice President elect shall act as President until a President shall have qualified; and the Congress may by law provide for the case wherein neither a President elect nor a Vice President shall have qualified, declaring who shall then act as President, or the manner in which one who is to act shall be selected, and such person shall act accordingly until a President or Vice President shall have qualified.

第十九条修正案

［1919 年 6 月 4 日提出，1920 年 8 月 18 日批准］

合众国公民的选举权，不得因性别而被合众国或任何一州加以拒绝或限制。

国会有权以适当立法实施本条。

第二十条修正案

［1933 年 3 月 2 日提出，1933 年 1 月 23 日批准］

第一款　总统和副总统的任期应在本条未获批准前原定任期届满之年的一月二十日正午结束，参议员和众议员的任期在本条未获批准前原定任期届满之年的一月三日正午结束，他们继任人的任期在同时开始。

第二款　国会每年至少应开会一次，除国会以法律另订日期外，此会议在一月三日正午开始。

第三款　如当选总统在规定总统任期开始的时间已经死亡，当选副总统应成为总统。如在规定总统任期开始的时间以前，总统尚未选出，或当选总统不合乎资格，则当选副总统应代理总统直到一名总统已合乎资格时为止。在当选总统和当选副总统都不合乎资格时，国会得以法律规定代理总统之人，或宣布选出代理总统的办法。此人应代理总统直到一名总统或副总统合乎资格时为止。

Section 4 The Congress may by law provide for the case of the death of any of the persons from whom the House of Representatives may choose a President whenever the right of choice shall have devolved upon them, and for the case of the death of any of the persons from whom the Senate may choose a Vice President whenever the right of choice shall have devolved upon them.

Section 5 Sections 1 and 2 shall take effect on the 15th day of October following the ratification of this article.

Section 6 This article shall be inoperative unless it shall have been ratified as an amendment to the Constitution by the legislatures of three-fourths of the several States within seven years from the date of its submission.

AMENDMENT XXI

Passed by Congress February 20, 1933. Ratified December 5, 1933.

Section 1 The eighteenth article of amendment to the Constitution of the United States is hereby repealed.

Section 2 The transportation or importation into any State, Territory, or Possession of the United States for delivery or use therein of intoxicating liquors, in violation of the laws thereof, is hereby prohibited.

Section 3 This article shall be inoperative unless it shall have been ratified as an amendment to the Constitution by conventions in the several States, as provided in the Constitution, within seven years from the date of the submission hereof to the States by the Congress.

AMENDMENT XXII

Passed by Congress March 21, 1947. Ratified February 27, 1951.

Section 1 No person shall be elected to the office of the President more than twice, and no person who has held the office of President, or acted as President, for more than two years of a term to which some other person was elected President shall be elected to the office of President more than once. But this Article shall not apply to any person holding the office of President when this Article was proposed by Congress, and shall not prevent any person who may be holding the office of President, or acting as President, during the term within which this Article becomes operative from holding the office of President or acting as President during the remainder of such term.

第四款　国会得以法律对以下情况作出规定：在选举总统的权利转移到众议院时，而可被该院选为总统的人中有人死亡；在选举副总统的权利转移到参议院时，而可被该院选为副总统的人中有人死亡。

第五款　第一款和第二款应在本条批准以后的十月十五日生效。

第六款　本条除非在其提交各州之日起七年以内，自四分之三州议会批准为宪法修正案，不得发生效力。

第二十一条修正案

［1933 年 2 月 20 日提出，1933 年 12 月 5 日批准］

第一款　美利坚合众国宪法修正案第十八条现予废除。

第二款　在合众国任何州、领地或属地内，凡违反当地法律为在当地发货或使用而运送或输入致醉酒类，均予以禁止。

第三款　本条除非在国会将其提交各州之日起七年以内，由各州制宪会议依本宪法规定批准为宪法修正案，不得发生效力。

第二十二条修正案

［1947 年 3 月 24 日提出，1951 年 2 月 27 日批准］

第一款　无论何人，当选担任总统职务不得超过两次；无论何人，在他人当选总统任期内担任总统职务或代理总统两年以上，不得当选担任总统职务一次以上。但本条不适用于在国会提出本条时正在担任总统职务的任何人；也不妨碍本条在一届总统任期内生效时正在担任总统职务或代理总统的任何人，在此届任期结束前继续担任总统职务或代理总统。

Section 2   This article shall be inoperative unless it shall have been ratified as an amendment to the Constitution by the legislatures of three-fourths of the several States within seven years from the date of its submission to the States by the Congress.

AMENDMENT XXIII

Passed by Congress June 16, 1960. Ratified March 29, 1961.

Section 1   The District constituting the seat of Government of the United States shall appoint in such manner as Congress may direct:

A number of electors of President and Vice President equal to the whole number of Senators and Representatives in Congress to which the District would be entitled if it were a State, but in no event more than the least populous State; they shall be in addition to those appointed by the States, but they shall be considered, for the purposes of the election of President and Vice President, to be electors appointed by a State; and they shall meet in the District and perform such duties as provided by the twelfth article of amendment.

Section 2   The Congress shall have power to enforce this article by appropriate legislation.

AMENDMENT XXIV

Passed by Congress August 27, 1962. Ratified January 23, 1964.

Section 1   The right of citizens of the United States to vote in any primary or other election for President or Vice President, for electors for President or Vice President, or for Senator or Representative in Congress, shall not be denied or abridged by the United States or any State by reason of failure to pay poll tax or other tax.

Section 2   The Congress shall have power to enforce this article by appropriate legislation.

AMENDMENT XXV

Passed by Congress July 6, 1965. Ratified February 10, 1967.

Note: Article II, section 1, of the Constitution was affected by the 25th amendment.

第二款　本条除非在国会将其提交各州之日起七年以内，由四分之三州议会批准为宪法修正案，不得发生效力。

第二十三条修正案
［1960 年 6 月 16 日提出，1961 年 3 月 29 日批准］

第一款　合众国政府所在的特区，应依国会规定方式选派：一定数目的总统和副总统选举人，其人数如同特区是一个州一样，等于它在国会有权拥有的参议员和众议员人数的总和，但不得超过人口最少之州的选举人人数。他们是在各州所选派的举人以外增添的人，但为了选举总统和副总统的目的，应被视为一个州选派的选举人；他们在特区集会，履行第十二条修正案所规定的职责。

第二款　国会有权以适当立法实施本条。

第二十四条修正案
［1962 年 8 月 27 日提出，1964 年 1 月 23 日批准］

第一款　合众国公民在总统或副总统、总统或副总统选举人、或国会参议员或众议员的任何预选或其他选举中的选举权，不得因未交纳任何人头税或其他税而被合众国或任何一州加以拒绝或限制。

第二款　国会有权以适当立法实施本条。

第二十五条修正案
［1965 年 7 月 6 日提出，1967 年 2 月 10 日批准］

Section 1   In case of the removal of the President from office or of his death or resignation, the Vice President shall become President.

Section 2   Whenever there is a vacancy in the office of the Vice President, the President shall nominate a Vice President who shall take office upon confirmation by a majority vote of both Houses of Congress.

Section 3   Whenever the President transmits to the President pro tempore of the Senate and the Speaker of the House of Representatives his written declaration that he is unable to discharge the powers and duties of his office, and until he transmits to them a written declaration to the contrary, such powers and duties shall be discharged by the Vice President as Acting President.

Section 4   Whenever the Vice President and a majority of either the principal officers of the executive departments or of such other body as Congress may by law provide, transmit to the President pro tempore of the Senate and the Speaker of the House of Representatives their written declaration that the President is unable to discharge the powers and duties of his office, the Vice President shall immediately assume the powers and duties of the office as Acting President.

Thereafter, when the President transmits to the President pro tempore of the Senate and the Speaker of the House of Representatives his written declaration that no inability exists, he shall resume the powers and duties of his office unless the Vice President and a majority of either the principal officers of the executive department or of such other body as Congress may by law provide, transmit within four days to the President pro tempore of the Senate and the Speaker of the House of Representatives their written declaration that the President is unable to discharge the powers and duties of his office. Thereupon Congress shall decide the issue, assembling within forty-eight hours for that purpose if not in session. If the Congress, within twenty-one days after receipt of the latter written declaration, or, if Congress is not in session, within twenty-one days after Congress is required to assemble, determines by two-thirds vote of both Houses that the President is unable to discharge the powers and duties of his office, the Vice President shall continue to discharge the same as Acting President; otherwise, the President shall resume the powers and duties of his office.

第一款　如遇总统被免职、死亡或辞职，副总统应成为总统。

第二款　凡当副总统职位出缺时，总统应提名一名副总统，经国会两院都以过半数票批准后就职。

第三款　凡当总统向参议院临时议长和众议院议长提交书面声明，声称他不能够履行其职务的权力和责任，直至他向他们提交一份相反的声明为止，其权力和责任应由副总统作为代理总统履行。

第四款　凡当副总统和行政各部长官的多数或国会以法律设立的其他机构成员的多数，向参议院临时议长和众议院议长提交书面声明，声称总统不能够履行总统职务的权力和责任时，副总统应立即作为代理总统承担总统职务的权力和责任。

此后，当总统向参议院临时议长和众议院议长提交书面声明，声称丧失能力的情况不存在时，他应恢复总统职务的权力和责任，除非副总统和行政各部长官的多数或国会以法律设立的其它机构成员的多数在四天之内向参议院临时议长和众议院议长提交书面声明，声称总统不能够履行总统职务的权力和责任。在此种情况下，国会应决定这一问题，如在休会期间，应为此目的在四十八小时以内集会。如国会在收到后一书面声明后的二十一天以内，或如适逢休会期间，则在国会按照要求集会以后的二十一天以内，以两院的三分之二的票数决定总统不能够履行总统职务的权力和责任，副总统应继续作为代理总统履行总统职务的权力和责任；否则总统应恢复总统职务的权力和责任。

AMENDMENT XXVI

Passed by Congress March 23, 1971. Ratified July 1, 1971.

Note: Amendment 14, section 2, of the Constitution was modified by section 1 of the 26th amendment.

Section 1   The right of citizens of the United States, who are eighteen years of age or older, to vote shall not be denied or abridged by the United States or by any State on account of age.

Section 2   The Congress shall have power to enforce this article by appropriate legislation.

AMENDMENT XXVII

Originally proposed Sept. 25, 1789. Ratified May 7, 1992.

No law, varying the compensation for the services of the Senators and Representatives, shall take effect, until an election of representatives shall have intervened.

第二十六条修正案

［1971 年 3 月 23 日提出，1971 年 7 月 1 日批准］

第一款　年满十八岁和十八岁以上的合众国公民的选举权，不得因为年龄而被合众国或任何一州加以拒绝或限制。

第二款　国会有权以适当立法实施本条。

第二十七条修正案

［1989 年 9 月 25 日提出，1992 年 5 月 7 日批准］

改变参议员和众议员服务报酬的法律，在众议员选举举行之前不得生效。

（本译本引用自李道揆《美国政府和美国政治》，商务印书馆，1999-03 版）

Reading for the Citizen of the World

世界公民读本（文库）

FOUNDATIONS of DEMOCRACY